Confronting Injustice and Oppression

Concepts and Strategies for Social Workers

Social Work Knowledge

Frederic G. Reamer, Series Editor

Social work has a unique history, purpose, perspective, and method. The primary purpose of this series is to articulate these distinct qualities and to define and explore the ideas, concepts, and skills that together constitute social work's intellectual foundations and boundaries and its emerging issues and concerns.

To accomplish this goal, the series will publish a cohesive collection of books that address both the core knowledge of the profession and its newly emerging topics. The core is defined by the evolving consensus, as primarily reflected in the Council of Social Work Education's Curriculum Policy Statement, concerning what courses accredited social work education programs must include in their curricula. The series will be characterized by an emphasis on the widely embraced ecological perspective; attention to issues concerning direct and indirect practice; and emphasis on cultural diversity and multiculturalism, social justice, oppression, populations at risk, and social work values and ethics. The series will have a dual focus on practice traditions and emerging issues and concepts.

Confronting Injustice and Oppression

Concepts and Strategies for Social Workers

by David G. Gil

Brandeis University

Columbia University Press

New York

Columbia University Press
Publishers Since 1893
New York   Chichester, West Sussex

Copyright © 1998 Columbia University Press

Library of Congress Cataloging-in-Publication Data
Gil, David G.
Confronting injustice and oppression : concepts and strategies
for social workers / by David G. Gill.
p.   cm. — (Social work knowledge)
Includes bibliographical references (p.   ) and index.
ISBN 0–231–10672–6 (cl : acid-free paper). — ISBN 0–231–10673–4 (pa)
1. Social justice. 2. Discrimination. 3. Social change. 4. Social service.
I. Title. II. Series.
HM216.G457 1998
303.3'72—dc21   97–30648
                                                                        CIP

∞

Casebound editions of Columbia University Press books are
printed on permanent and durable acid-free paper.
Printed in the United States of America
c 10 9 8 7 6 5 4 3 2 1
p 10 9 8 7 6 5 4 3 2 1

To Eva, my partner in life and work.

To teachers, students, colleagues, and friends,
near and far in time and place,
whose thoughts and practice
this book reflects;

To people everywhere
who pursue community
where all are equal and free
and human potential can flourish.

CONTENTS

ACKNOWLEDGMENTS

I would not have written this book unless Professor Frederic G. Reamer, the editor of the Social Work Knowledge Series, had offered me an opportunity to sum up my insights into injustice, oppression, and social change. I am grateful to him for urging me to accept this assignment, for it enabled me to develop and present my thoughts more systematically than I had done in separate publications in the past.

I would also like to thank my editors at Columbia University Press, John Michel and Alexander Thorp, as well as the reviewers of my manuscript, for their support throughout the writing of this book. Finally, my thanks go to the editorial, design, desktopping, and marketing staffs of Columbia University Press, and to Auralie Logan, who made the Index.

Confronting Injustice and Oppression

Concepts and Strategies for Social Workers

INTRODUCTION

The Relevance of Injustice and Oppression
for Social Work and Social Policy

Social workers and social policy professionals have always been involved with victims of injustice and oppression. Yet, though they tend to grasp intuitively and emotionally the meaning of these dehumanizing conditions, they usually lack theoretical insights into their causes, and into strategies to transform unjust and oppressive social, economic, and political institutions into just and nonoppressive alternatives. To close such a gap in social work knowledge, this book aims to develop theoretical insights concerning:

- the sources and dynamics of injustice and oppression;
- strategies for social change to overcome injustice and oppression; and
- implications of these insights for social work practice and social policy development and advocacy.

These insights seem essential to effective practice of social workers and social policy analysts and advocates, as most issues they have dealt with in the past, and are dealing with now, are directly or indirectly related to the dynamics and conditions of injustice and oppression.

In exploring these theoretical, historical, strategic, and practice issues, the book addresses the ethical, professional, and educational mandates expressed or implied in the Code of Ethics of the National Association of Social Workers (NASW), the International Declaration of Ethical Principles of Social Work of the International Federation of Social Workers (IFSW), and the Curriculum Policy Statement of the Council on Social Work Education (CSWE) for graduate and under-graduate social work education. Relevant statements from these policy documents are quoted below:

> NASW Code of Ethics, 1996
> Value: Social Justice
> Ethical Principle: Social workers challenge social injustice

Social workers pursue social change, particularly with and on behalf of vulnerable and oppressed individuals and groups of people. . . .

> Social Workers' Ethical Responsibilities to the Broader Society

Social workers should act to prevent and eliminate domination of, exploitation of, and discrimination against any person, group, or class on the basis of race, ethnicity, national origin, color, sex, sexual orientation, age, marital status, political belief, religion, or mental or physical disability.

> IFSW, 1994
> Principles

Social workers have a commitment to principles of social justice.

Social workers respect the basic human rights of individuals and groups as expressed in the United Nations Universal Declaration of Human Rights and other international conventions derived from that Declaration (see appendix B).

> CSWE, 1994
> Promotion of social and economic justice

Programs of social work education must provide an understanding of the dynamics and consequences of social and economic injustice, including all forms of human oppression and discrimination. They must provide students with the skills to promote social change and to implement a wide range of interventions that further the achievement of individual and collective social and economic justice. Theoretical and practice content must be provided about strategies of intervention for achieving social and economic justice and for combating the causes and effects of institutionalized forms of oppression.

Overview

The book is divided into two parts: part 1 presents theoretical and historical perspectives; part 2 addresses implications for policy development, social work practice and education, and empowerment and organizing of social-justice-oriented social workers.

More specifically, part 1 analyzes the meaning of injustice and oppression, as well as of justice and freedom from oppression. It unravels links and interactions among societal processes and conditions these concepts refer to, and traces their origins, evolution, dynamics, and consequences.

Part 1 discusses also theories and strategies for the transformation of social, economic, political, and cultural institutions that obstruct human development into alternatives conducive to human development and liberation. In discussing social change, the important, yet often overlooked, differences between short-term and long-term goals and corresponding strategies are being clarified. Fundamental social change is conceived not as brief, cataclysmic events, but as long-term processes, involving comprehensive cultural and institutional transformations, which depend on prior major changes of people's consciousness and values. In discussing nonviolent versus violent social change strategies, the concepts *social-structural violence*, *counterviolence*, and *repressive violence* are clarified, and their sources, dynamics, and consequences are traced.

The discussion in chapters 1 to 3 may seem rather abstract to some readers and not *directly* relevant to social workers' everyday practice. Please be patient as you read and think about this material. This analysis of key concepts is necessary to discern the universal dynamics of injustice and oppression, and to avoid dealing with their different manifestations in contemporary society, such as racism, sexism, class domination, etc., as separate phenomena with supposedly separate solutions. Insights developed through the theoretical analyses in these chapters will facilitate the subsequent discussion of themes relevant to social work and social services.

Part 1 concludes with sketches of important phases in the development of social work which reveal that, while social workers have usually helped people to live with, and adjust to, conditions of injustice and oppression by alleviating their symptoms, they have also addressed causes of injustice, and have helped people to resist oppression, and to organize for empowerment and liberation. Illustrations are provided of symptom-alleviating, as well as of system-challenging, tendencies in social work.

Part 2 begins with a discussion of feasible *transition policies* designed to eliminate poverty, unemployment, and discrimination, even prior to attaining the long-term objectives of social and economic justice and liberty from oppression.

Central to part 2 is an exploration of implications of commitments to social and economic justice for social work practice and education, and for social policy development and advocacy. Illustrations are used from direct clinical practice and social work education, and from social policy development and advocacy. The purpose of these illustrations is to differentiate between adjustment-oriented, status-quo-maintaining approaches, and social-change-oriented, alternative approaches, involving challenges to injustice and oppression.

Part 2 concludes with a discussion of support-and-study groups of social-change-oriented social workers, and networks of such groups. Such groups could facilitate empowerment and organizing, through collective study of social-justice-oriented practice, in nonhierarchical, noncompetitive, egalitarian contexts.

The Epilogue presents reflections on insights gained, and their relevance for human survival and development.

Assumptions

Several assumptions underlie the following explorations of injustice and oppression.

- Relations of domination and exploitation within and among human societies, whenever and wherever they exist, and unjust ways of life enforced and shaped by such relations, are results of human choices and actions. While not contrary to human nature, oppression and injustice are not inevitable expressions of it. This assumption is supported by the existence, throughout history, of human groups and entire societies, whose internal and external relations were shaped by values of equality, liberty, solidarity, and cooperation rather than by dynamics of domination, exploitation and injustice (Kropotkin 1956; Maslow and Honigman 1970).

- Societies that initiated relations of domination and exploitation and conditions of injustice, on small scales and local levels, tended to extend these relations and conditions also beyond their populations and territories. Such oppressive practices and tendencies intensified gradually and acquired momentum as a result of cycles of resistance by victims and reactive repression by perpetrators, as well as through competition for dominance among different oppressive and unjust societies. Eventually, relations of domination and exploitation, and conditions of injustice, penetrated and permeated most branches of humankind all over the globe.

- Relations of domination and exploitation and conditions of injustice, and the coercive processes by which they were established, maintained, and extended within and beyond societies, came to be reflected not only in social, economic, cultural, and political institutions, and in all spheres of everyday life, but also in the consciousness and behavior of their victims and perpetrators.

- Relations of domination and exploitation, and conditions of injustice, and their gradual expansion were never, nor are they now, inevitable. People have often challenged these destructive practices and conditions, and are likely to do so again, by organizing liberation movements and spreading critical consciousness—a prerequisite for collective action toward fundamental social change (Freire 1970). Such movements have usually encountered overt and covert resistance from social classes committed to conserve ways of life they consider compatible with their perceived needs and interests. While the outcomes of conflicts between challengers and defenders of oppression and injustice cannot be known, struggles for human liberation will, and should, go on. Social workers can and should take part in these struggles through their practice and everyday lives (Gil 1974).

Roots of the Work and Potential Bias

The emotional and intellectual roots of this work reach far back to my childhood experiences of injustice and oppression, following the German occupation of Austria in 1938. A traumatic separation from my home and family at age fourteen, when my father was imprisoned in a concentration camp, led me to raise a crucial question, which I have tried to answer ever since: "How can injustice and oppression be overcome and prevented, regardless of who the victims are?" In pursuing this question, I was not interested in retribution against particular perpetrators of oppression, including my own, but in reversing the vicious circles of violence. My quest led me eventually to a philosophy and practice of social equality, equal liberty, individuality in community, cooperation, and active nonviolence. The present work is part of this quest and reflects this philosophical bias (Buber 1958; Freire 1970; King 1992; Kropotkin 1956; Sharp 1973, 1979; Tawney 1964).

PART ONE

Theoretical and Historical Perspectives

I

Injustice and Oppression:
Meaning, Links, and Alternatives

As noted in the Introduction, social workers are required by their Code of Ethics "to challenge social injustice," and "to prevent and eliminate domination of, exploitation of, and discrimination against any person, group, or class." The Code does not specify, however, the meanings of these terms, as if they were self-evident. Yet social justice cannot be promoted, nor can oppression, domination, exploitation, and social injustice be overcome, unless their meanings, sources, and dynamics are clarified.

Unraveling these meanings, sources, and dynamics is, however, fraught with difficulties, mainly because oppression tends to be more effective in achieving its ends—enforcement of domination, exploitation, social injustice, and constraints on liberty—when people are not conscious of the societal dynamics involved, when victims and victimizers perceive these conditions as natural and inevitable, and, especially, when the victims share illusions of being free citizens of a democracy. Throughout much of human history, denial and rationalization of oppression and injustice, and their validation as sacred and secular law and order, may actually have been the most effective means in the defense and legitimation of unjust ways of life which tended to benefit mainly powerful and privileged social groups and classes.

Students of injustice and oppression, and of their opposites need, therefore, to explore not only the meanings, sources, and dynamics of these phenomena, but also their own consciousness and values, their possible direct and indirect benefits from, and denials of, injustice and oppression, as well as their unexamined, taken-for-granted justifications of established, oppressive and unjust ways of life.

Meaning of Injustice and Oppression and Their Opposites

Oppression refers to a mode of human relations involving domination and exploitation—economic, social, and psychologic—between individuals; between social groups and classes within and beyond societies; and, globally, between entire societies. Injustice refers to coercively established and maintained inequalities, discrimination, and dehumanizing, development-inhibiting conditions of living (e.g., slavery, serfdom, and exploitative wage labor; unemployment, poverty, starvation, and homelessness; inadequate health care and education), imposed by dominant social groups, classes, and peoples upon dominated and exploited groups, classes, and peoples.

Domination is usually motivated by the intent to exploit (i.e., benefit disproportionally from the resources, capacities, labor, and productivity of others), and it results typically in disadvantageous, unjust conditions of living for its victims. Domination is the *means* to enforce exploitation toward the *end* of attaining and maintaining privileged conditions of living for certain social groups relative to some other groups. Justice is the absence of exploitation-enforcing domination; it implies liberty, while domination-induced injustice involves unequal, discriminatory constraints on liberty.

To individuals, groups, classes, and peoples who dominate and exploit others, and impose upon them unjust conditions of living, these policies and practices tend to make sense. For in the consciousness of people involved in relations of oppression, their attitudes and actions seem, by and large, compatible with law and order, i.e., the pursuit of socially sanctioned, legitimate goals, and with the internal logic of established social, cultural, economic, and political institutions. How and why did human societies evolve ways of life in which oppression and injustice came to be taken for granted and considered legitimate and appropriate? Answers to this disturbing question are being developed in chapter 2.

Societies whose internal and external relations involve oppressive tendencies are usually not divided simply into oppressors and oppressed people. Rather, people in such societies tend to be oppressed in some relations and oppressors in others, while some relations may involve mutual oppression. Oppression is not a static context but a dynamic process. Once integrated into a society's institutional order and culture, and into the individual consciousness of its people through socialization, oppressive tendencies come to permeate and affect almost all relations. Oppression thus tends to evolve into hierarchical chains and vicious circles. The intensity of oppression is, however, not constant but varies over time as a result of countertendencies toward human solidarity, which tend to give rise to liberation movements struggling to overcome oppression (Freire 1970).

Defining Characteristics of Injustice and Oppression and Their Opposites

To discern the defining characteristics of injustice and oppression, and of their opposites, one needs to examine how just and nonoppressive, and how unjust and oppressive human relations are shaped by the following key institutions of social life and their underlying values:

a. stewardship (i.e., development, management, control, use, and ownership) of natural and human-created resources;
b. organization of work and production;
c. exchange of products of human work, and distribution (i.e., indirect exchange) of concrete and symbolic goods and services, and of social, civil, and political rights and responsibilities;
d. governance and legitimation;
e. biological reproduction, socialization, and social control.

In any human group, at any time, the combined effects of these key institutions of social life, and of the values underlying them, shape the circumstances of living and the relative power of individuals, social groups, and classes; the quality of human relations among individuals, groups, and classes; and the overall quality of life, be these relations and conditions nonoppressive and just or oppressive and unjust (Gil 1992).

By focusing the analysis of oppression, injustice, and their opposites on these key institutions and the values underlying them, I do not mean to disregard other social, psychological, historical, and cultural dimensions of social relations and living conditions. I merely intend to stress that, regardless of the role such other dimensions may play in maintaining and reproducing these relations and conditions, injustice and oppression can neither be understood, nor overcome at their roots, apart from the institutions of resource stewardship, work and production, exchange and distribution, governance and legitimation, and reproduction, socialization, and social control. For these institutions, and the social values which shape them, constitute always the very core of any mode of social life. The manner of operation of these key institutions would, therefore, have to be changed significantly, if an oppressive and unjust mode of life is to be transformed into its opposite.

Furthermore, resource use, work, exchange, and reproduction, seem to be fundamental processes, not only of human social organization, but of all forms of life in nature. Living beings, from single cells to complex organisms, are never self-contained, but assure their existence by interacting with other organisms and nonorganic substances in their environments. This is how they generate, obtain, and transmit matter and energy necessary for individual and species survival. These essential, life-sustaining interactions in nature may be understood as the universal model of resource use, work, exchange, and reproduction. Organisms that cease to engage in such life-sustaining interactions are dying. Resource-use, work, exchange, and reproduction seem, therefore, a sine qua non of all life, and their organization and institutionalization are essential for human survival and societal continuity. In the case of the human species, governance and legitimation, i.e., processes of making and legitimating choices and decisions, must be added to the list of essential institutional systems. Accordingly, systems of resource stewardship, work, exchange, governance, and reproduction are valid foci for the analysis of oppression and injustice, as well as for efforts to overcome these dehumanizing practices and conditions.

Stewardship of resources, work and production, exchange and distribution, governance and legitimation, and reproduction, socialization, and social control can be, and have actually been, organized by different societies, in different times and circumstances, in nonoppressive and just ways, in accordance with values of equality, liberty, mutualism, cooperation, and community. Conversely, they can be, and have been, organized in oppressive and unjust ways, in accordance with values of inequality, domination, exploitation, competition, and selfishness (i.e., disregard for others and community).

Based on the foregoing considerations, the defining characteristics of nonoppressive and oppressive societies and of just and unjust systems of exchange and distribution can now be identified:

Societies are nonoppressive: when all people are considered and treated as equals, and, therefore, have equal rights and responsibilities concerning:

- stewardship and use of resources;
- control, organization, design, substance, quality, and scope of production; and the amount and type of work they perform;
- exchange and distribution of goods and services, and of social, civil, and political rights and responsibilities;
- governance of their communities and society, and
- biological reproduction, socialization, and social control.

Under such genuinely democratic conditions, everyone would enjoy the same level of liberty, and would be subject to the same level of expectations and constraints concerning work and other aspects of life.

Societies are oppressive: when people are not considered and treated as equals, and, therefore, do not have equal rights and responsibilities concerning the key institutions of social life. Under such inherently undemocratic conditions, different people, and different groups and classes, are entitled to different levels of liberty, and are subject to different levels of expectations and constraints concerning work and other aspects of life. Establishing and maintaining unequal levels of rights and responsibilities concerning the key institutions of social life, and unequal levels of liberty, expectations, and constraints concerning work, is usually not possible without overt and covert domination and coercion, i.e., "societal violence" (Gil 1992, 1996).

Systems of exchange and distribution are just:

- when terms of exchange (measured in units of human work and natural and human-created resources invested in the products of differ-

ent workers), are fair and balanced, i.e., egalitarian and nonexploitative;
- when everyone's individual needs and potential are considered and
  treated as equally important; and
- when all people are treated as equals, relative to their individual
  needs, in the distribution of concrete and symbolic goods and services and social, civil, political, and reproductive rights and responsibilities; and with regard to socialization experiences and opportunities (Barry 1973; Rawls 1971; Tawney 1964).

Systems of exchange and distribution are unjust:

- when terms of exchange are discriminatory, unfair, and unbalanced,
  i.e., unequal and exploitative;
- when the needs and potential of members of certain groups and
  classes are deemed more important than those of others; and
- when these individuals, groups, and classes receive routinely prefer-
  ential treatment, relative to others, in the distribution of concrete and
  symbolic goods and services, and of social, civil, political, and reproductive rights and responsibilities, and with regard to socialization
  experiences and opportunities.

Establishing and maintaining unjust modes of exchange and distribution are usually predicated upon overt and covert processes of coercion and domination, in the same way as establishing and maintaining
oppressive social orders and work systems.

Oppression and injustice tend to vary among societies in levels of
intensity, from very low to very high. These variations reflect differences in values and in degrees of inequality with respect to the key
institutions of social life in particular societies at particular times. The
higher the degrees of inequality, the higher also are likely to be the levels of coercion necessary to enforce inequality, as well as the levels of
conflict, resistance, and reactive repression.

It may be noted here, that an important function of social work and
social services throughout history has been to modify and fine-tune the
intensity of oppression and injustice in societies, and to ameliorate
their destructive consequences for human development. Social work
and social services were, however, never meant to eliminate inequalities, oppression and injustice, and their consequences.

While variations are possible in the levels of intensity of oppression and injustice, variations are not possible concerning social justice and nonoppressive relations, which, by definition, are predicated upon equal rights and responsibilities with regard to the key institutions of social life. Equal rights and responsibilities can not vary by levels, because equality is not a continuum, but the zero point on the continuum of inequality.

When politicians and social work leaders, in public policy discourse, nevertheless advocate "more equality," as they often do illogically, what they actually mean are lower levels of inequality, privilege, and deprivation, but not real social equality and elimination of discrimination, privilege, and deprivation. Reductions of inequality, discrimination, privilege, and deprivation are, of course, improvements in the quality of social life, but should not be mistaken for an end to oppression and the establishment of justice. The quality of social life will continue to be affected by the dynamics and logic of oppression and injustice, as long as some level of inequality concerning the key institutions of social life will be conserved, and dominant social values will remain essentially unchanged.

Historically, societies which developed nonoppressive social orders and work systems tended also to evolve just systems of exchange and distribution, while societies which developed oppressive social orders and work systems tended to evolve unjust systems of exchange and distribution. These typical associations between nonoppressive social orders and work systems and just systems of exchange and distribution, on the one hand, and oppressive and unjust ones on the other, reflect causal links between oppression and injustice, and nonoppressive social relations and justice.

These associations suggest and reflect also the presence or absence of overt and covert coercion or societal violence, which has been used throughout history, and continues to be used in our time, by dominant groups, classes, and peoples, from local to global levels, in order to establish, maintain, and legitimate privileged conditions of living for themselves. People have always been unlikely to submit of their own free will to discriminatory, development-inhibiting, inegalitarian practices concerning the key institutions of social life. Accordingly, it does not seem possible to ever establish and maintain such systems and conditions of living through truly democratic processes, and without at least some measure of overt and covert coercion or societal violence.

It follows from these theoretical considerations that whenever significant inequalities are prevalent in a society concerning the key institutions of social life, such as unemployment, relative poverty, hunger and homelessness, inadequate education and health care, and distinctions and discrimination by social class, race, sex, sexual orientation, age, and disabilities—the gamut of conditions that bring people to social services—its ways of life involve oppression and injustice; its people are not free in a meaningful sense; and its political institutions are essentially undemocratic, coercive, and structurally violent, in spite of formal elections and misleading claims, such as "being part of the free world."

2

Injustice and Oppression:
Origins, Evolution, Dynamics, and Consequences

Historical Notes

Contrary to widely held, taken-for-granted beliefs, injustice and oppression are not inevitable, natural characteristics of human life. The study of social evolution reveals that these practices did not become firmly established in human societies until some ten thousand years ago, following the discovery, development, and spread of agriculture, animal husbandry, and crafts, which gradually generated a stable economic surplus. These new conditions facilitated the emergence of complex divisions of work, of occupational and social castes and classes, and of spatial and social differentiations of societies into rural peasant communities and urban centers. Since homo sapiens, the species of modern humans is thought to have evolved more than two hundred thousand years ago, the last ten thousand years are a relatively short period, and should not be perceived erroneously as our entire history (Eisler 1987).

For many millennia, from the emergence of the early humans until the agricultural revolution, people tended to live in small and isolated nomadic communities that subsisted by gathering, fishing, and hunting. The internal organization of these societies was usually based on egalitarian, cooperative, and communal principles, and did not involve systematic oppression, exploitation, and injustice.

People's resources during these early stages of evolution consisted of their human capacities, their accumulated experiences and orally transmitted knowledge and traditions, and the natural wealth of the territories they inhabited. Stewardship over these resources was exercised collectively toward the goal of meeting everyone's survival needs. Work roles were barely differentiated, as nearly everyone had to participate in securing the basic necessities for survival. Whatever division of work did emerge tended to be based on age, sex, physical conditions, and individual capacities, but not, as during later stages of social evolution, on discriminatory social criteria, such as tribe, race, religion, caste, or class.

Exchanges of work products and the distribution of goods and services tended to be balanced and egalitarian, i.e., nonexploitative. In the course of their lives, most people contributed to, and received from, aggregate social production about as much as others. Social, civil, and political rights and responsibilities also tended to be shared equally and to be linked to age, sex, and capacities. People enjoyed roughly equal liberties, and they were subject to roughly equal constraints, concerning work and reproduction.

These essentially egalitarian modes of resource stewardship, work and production, exchange and distribution, governance, socialization, and reproduction seem to have required little coercion beyond child rearing and conformity-inducing public opinion. For, under conditions prevailing in these early societies, people seem to have been self-motivated to work, as their work was typically linked directly to their real interests, the satisfaction of their basic needs.

Levels of conflict within societies seem to have been low during the early stages of evolution, as everyone's needs were deemed equally important, and were met accordingly, subject to limits set by the resources and the collective productivity of societies. Also, since the gathering, hunting, and fishing mode of production necessitated nearly everyone's participation to assure provisions for basic needs, few opportunities existed for the emergence of crafts and the generation of a stable economic surplus—the disposition and appropriation of which became a potential source of conflicts during later stages of social evolution.

Finally, apart from their egalitarian, cooperative, and communal value premises, the actual ways of life of early human societies were not conducive to establishing systems of economic exploitation such as slavery, serfdom, or exploitative wage labor. Their simple technologies, typically, did not enable people to produce, in the course of their lives, significantly more than they consumed for their subsistence. They were, therefore, unable to generate a stable economic surplus for appropriation and exploitation by others—the material basis and precondition for the emergence of systems of oppression.

I do not mean to idealize here the ways of life of early human groups, nor to advocate a return to that primeval stage of social evolution, in order to overcome oppression and injustice in contemporary societies. I also do not suggest that human relations were then free from oppressive tendencies, especially in relations between men and women, between older and younger persons, and between members of societies and strangers they encountered. I am also aware that relations between different societies were not always peaceful then.

However, from what has been learned by anthropology, archaeology, and history about this very long, preagricultural and preliterate period of human evolution, oppression, and injustice in relation to the key institutions of social life, as perpetrated routinely by many societies over the past ten millennia, were not institutionalized policies and practices. We could, therefore, derive important insights from the values and ways of life of early human communities, and enhance thus our ability to overcome oppression and injustice in contemporary societies.

What conditions and forces have brought about radical transformations of the relatively static, continuously self-reproducing, traditional patterns of life of early human societies? Likely answers to this important historical question are implicit in the existential imperative of the human condition to assure a steady flow of suitable, life-sustaining necessities from a society's environment, while conserving also that environment's regenerative capacities. Humans must always maintain a rough balance between their survival needs and their abilities to satisfy these needs in particular environments, given their particular levels of scientific and technological development. This essential balance may be upset by unchecked population increases relative to the carrying capacity of a society's territory. When such imbalances occurred and reached critical levels, human groups could not survive and continue living in their traditional ways unless they expanded their territories or migrated to different ones. Survival could also be assured by discovering and developing new technologies and new ways of life that enabled people to reestablish an adequate balance between their growing numbers, needs, and environmental resources.

Many early human communities, whose population increases were insignificant for a long time, eventually experienced accelerated increases in their numbers, which did upset the essential balance between them and their environments. Some of these societies, in different parts of the globe, at about the same time (some eight to ten millennia ago), overcame the threats to their survival by discovering and developing agriculture and animal husbandry, and initiating thereby a new era of social development with new challenges, opportunities, choices, and risks.

The introduction of agriculture and animal husbandry had revolutionary consequences for the ways of life of nomadic societies which developed them, and for their internal and external relations. Gradually, they began to establish sedentary peasant communities that were able to generate a relatively reliable and ample food supply. Because of this increase in productivity, it was no longer necessary for everyone to engage in food production, and growing numbers of people could, henceforth, pursue alternative occupations and roles. In time, this led to divisions between manual and mental work, and to the emergence of social and occupational castes and classes, including peasants, artisans, and traders; priests, scholars, professionals, and artists; civilian administrators, soldiers, and ruling elites. Occupational differentiations and specializations led gradually also to spatial differentiations—the emergence of cities and neighborhoods—and to social, economic, political, and cultural differentiations, all of which resulted in differences in ways of life, consciousness, perceived interests, values, and ideologies among subgroups of societies.

These multifaceted developments reflect a gradual transformation, following the spread of agriculture, of the egalitarian, cooperative, and communal ways of life of hunting and gathering societies, into alternative systems. The new systems involved tendencies toward expropri-

ation, fragmentation, and concentration concerning resource stewardship, and increasingly complex divisions of labor, which began to yield
a significant economic surplus—the material base and precondition
for the emergence of domination, exploitation, and injustice. These
changes concerning resource stewardship and work and production
led also to corresponding significant changes in modes of exchange and
distribution, and in overall social organization, values, and ideologies.
Illustrations of these developments are the ancient civilizations of
Mesopotamia and Egypt (Durant 1935; Garraty and Gay 1972).

To be sure, these developments took centuries and millennia, and
involved, at any stage, many choices, none of which were ever
inevitable. Indeed, different societies, which developed agriculture and
animal husbandry in different regions of the globe, at different times,
made different choices and developed different patterns of resource
stewardship, division of work, and exchange and distribution, which
also gave rise to different sets of values and ideologies.

Before tracing the emergence and institutionalization of domination, exploitation, and injustice—the most widespread consequence of
the agricultural revolution—it is important to note that not all societies
that developed agriculture developed systems of oppression. Some
societies used the economic surplus resulting from their increased productivity toward enhancing the quality of life for all their members,
and they continued to manage resources, to organize work and production, and exchange and distribution in accordance with egalitarian,
cooperative, and communal values. Illustrations of this tendency have
been identified by anthropologists and historians among native peoples
in America, Africa, and elsewhere. Many of these native societies preserved essentially nonoppressive and just ways of life until, and often
beyond, the violent conquests of their lands by colonizing European
empires (Farb 1968; Zinn 1980).

The ways by which oppression and injustice were established as
dominant modes of social life, following the development of agriculture, have varied among societies. Two main related and interacting
types may be distinguished:

- exploiting strangers, i.e., other societies and their people and
  resources; and
- exploiting fellow citizens within societies.

Historically, societies that have practiced exploitation and oppression have usually done so at home and abroad, as both types involve
similar assumptions, value premises, and ideologies, and as internal
and external human relations interact with, and influence, one another.
It is nevertheless useful to differentiate conceptually between external
and internal exploitation and oppression, and to analyze their emergence separately, since they do differ in origins.

Exploiting and Oppressing Strangers

Agricultural products ripening in the fields of societies that had preceded others in developing this new mode of production and survival
attracted preagricultural societies to invade peasant settlements to
appropriate their products, especially when population increases were
threatening the food supply of the invaders. These invasions were the
beginnings of warfare between societies, motivated by efforts to
achieve control over economic resources. Invasions of ancient
European peasant communities by Asian nomadic tribes, the Kurgans,
illustrate this process (Eisler 1987).

While these violent encounters probably made sense in the consciousness of those involved, in spite of high costs in human life, they
were clearly not inevitable. The discoverers of agriculture may have
been ready to share their knowledge, technology, and skills peacefully
with others, as native peoples have actually done in the Americas when
European explorers and conquerors first arrived.

The invasions of peasant communities around harvest time resulted
gradually in their coercive enslavement by nomadic peoples, who
became accustomed to securing their food supplies by appropriating
the fruits of other people's work, and who apparently preferred living
by marauding to acquiring agricultural technologies in order to produce their own food. Invasions to appropriate the products of peasant
communities did initially not result in enslavement, as the invaders
tended to kill many people of the invaded communities. However, with
time they realized the advantage of keeping the people alive, and coercing them to continue raising crops, and to turn over much of their
products to the invaders as tribute, in acknowledgement of submission.
Eventually, nomadic invaders not only coerced conquered communi-

ties to continue farming and turning over their surplus products but also captured people from the conquered communities, and enslaved and exploited them sexually in the captors' own communities.

One can identify the typical elements of oppression and injustice in these early relationships between nomadic warrior peoples and peasant communities, over whom they gained dominance coercively, and whom they subsequently enslaved. The motivating factor of the interaction is economic exploitation of the resources and productive capacities of conquered people. This is accomplished by gaining control over their basic resources—their territories—and forcing them to perform labor that the dominant society is not doing for itself, and to turn over the surplus product of this work, exclusive of what is necessary for the subsistence of the dominated and enslaved communities.

With time, social, psychological, and ideological dimensions evolved around the economic roots of oppressive and exploitative relationships: the prestige of labor performed by the enslaved people (agriculture) declined relative to the prestige of activities engaged in by the dominant people (military and governance functions), regardless of the objective importance of the work and activities; and the status and prestige of dominated, enslaved workers declined relative to that of members of dominant societies. These perceptions of the relative value, status, and prestige of work and workers became internalized in the consciousness of everyone involved in exploitative and oppressive relations, and they became the core of discriminatory ideologies and practices concerning different occupations, social groups, castes, classes, and peoples. Phenomena such as classism, occupational hierarchies, sexism, racism, ethnocentrism, and so forth, are contemporary manifestations and expressions of these ancient tendencies.

Imposing oppressive relations and unjust conditions on other societies in order to exploit their natural resources, the potential of their people to work, and their human-created goods and services, as was done on relatively small scales by marauding nomadic peoples following the agricultural revolution, has gradually become the model for establishing colonies and empires during antiquity, the Middle Ages, and modern times. Details have varied from case to case, but institutional practices have remained essentially the same throughout the history of conquest and colonialism, and so have the social, psychologi-

cal, and ideological dimensions, as well as the secular and religious justifications for exploitation, oppression, injustice, and discrimination
(Frank 1977; Magdoff 1977).

Exploiting and Oppressing Fellow Citizens

Oppression and injustice emerged, following the spreading of agriculture, within many, but not all, societies, as a possible consequence of
occupational, social, and spatial differentiations. Whether or not these
differentiations resulted in oppressive relations and unjust conditions
seems to have depended largely on the terms of exchange that were
established between peasants in rural communities and people pursuing newly emerging crafts and other occupations and roles, mainly in
urban centers.

If exchanges were just, i.e., fairly balanced, in terms of human and
material resources invested in respective products and services, then
relations between a society's peasantry and social groups pursuing
other occupations, and living mainly in cities, could evolve along voluntary, noncoercive, nonoppressive, and synergetic patterns, with
everyone benefiting equally (Maslow and Honigman 1970).

If, on the other hand, exchanges were unjust, i.e., imbalanced,
establishment and maintenance of such conditions required typically
physical and ideological coercion, that is, oppression or societal violence. In these situations, urban dwellers were bent upon exploiting the
peasantry, and gradually also each other, as occupational specializations and social differentiations multiplied, and as each occupational
and social group or class aspired to appropriate as much as possible of
the aggregate economic surplus by consistently claiming, and struggling for, privileged shares of available goods and services.

Unjust and oppressive societies, which are based on coercively
maintained exploitative exchanges among people and classes engaging
in different occupations and performing different social roles and
enjoying different levels of rights, responsibility, and liberty, were not
as stable and change-resistant as preagricultural, egalitarian, cooperative, and communal societies. They were changing continuously as a
result of gradually intensifying competition and conflicts among individuals and social and occupational groups, who gained control over

different shares of resources and different roles in the work system, and who consequently were able to command different shares in the distribution of goods and services, and civil and political rights and power.

During early stages of the emergence of unjust and oppressive relations, following the establishment of societies based on agriculture and crafts, the egalitarian, cooperative, and communal values, ideology, and consciousness of preagricultural societies were gradually transformed into their opposites. These value changes toward inequality, competition, and selfishness were conducive to the ongoing development and stabilization of occupationally, spatially, and socially fragmented and stratified societies.

Once inequalities concerning resources, social and occupational roles, and goods, services, and rights were established in a society, they tended to be perpetuated, since individuals and groups who controlled disproportionally larger shares of resources and access to preferred work were in advantageous positions to assure continuation of these privileges, and even to increase them. Also, emerging legal and political institutions tended to reflect prevailing societal inequalities and differences of power among competing interest groups and classes, and were therefore unlikely to upset temporary equilibria among them.

The processes, dynamics, and logic of conflict and competition within societies apparently originated in minor initial inequalities in exchanges among individuals and occupational and social groups, which barely required coercion. However, the emerging tendency to legitimate, institutionalize, and increase initial, minimal inequalities did require coercion. This resulted usually in resistance from victimized groups, to which privileged groups reacted with intensified coercion. The vicious circle of domination and exploitation, resistance, and repression intensified with time, as people tended to focus on, and to react to, the latest violent stage in the circle, but did not trace the sources of their destructive interactions. They lacked, therefore, insights to reverse their course, and to move in alternative, constructive, nonexploitative directions.

It may be difficult to accept that minimal, initial inequalities within human societies, concerning the key institutions of social life, have led eventually to contemporary, massive, and still expanding inequalities within and among societies. While analogies do not prove anything, it may nevertheless be of interest to reflect on the latest hypotheses, and supportive discoveries, of cosmology, according to which massive galactic structures evolved out of minimal variations in densities and temperatures in the smooth physical medium of the early, expanding universe.

The tendency for inequalities to intensify in societies, once they are initiated on a small scale, has important implications for social workers and others who advocate reductions rather than elimination of inequalities: as long as inequalities, at any level, are considered legitimate and are being enforced by governments, competitive interactions focused on restructuring inequalities tend to continue among individuals, social groups, and classes, and a genuine sense of community and solidarity is unlikely to evolve.

One reason for the constant intensification of coercion in unjust and oppressive societies was that the motivation of people to work declined in proportion to the increase in exploitation. Work discipline had, therefore, to be assured by ever more overt and covert coercion. Hypocritical expectations concerning a work ethic became typical elements of socialization, and of religions and ideologies which interpreted and justified established, unequal conditions of life and work. In turn, socialization and indoctrination had to be routinely backed up by elaborate systems of submission-inducing rewards and sanctions, and by systems of social control, involving open and secret police and military forces, the instruments of legitimate violence within inegalitarian societies, and among societies of unjust and exploitative global systems.

The long history of the origins and development of oppression and injustice within and among societies over the past ten thousand years is essentially a series of variations on the theme of coercively initiated and maintained exploitative modes of resource control, work and production, exchange and distribution, and governance and socialization. This history is a tragic one indeed. The mere mention of coercive work systems such as ancient and recent slavery, feudal serfdom, and early and contemporary industrial and agricultural exploitative wage labor, brings to mind images of toiling people transformed, not by their own choice, into dehumanized factors of production, dominated and exploited by tyrants and slave masters, absolute rulers and aristocrats, and individual and corporate, capitalist employers. Such work systems could never have been established and perpetuated without massive coercion and violence in the form of civil and foreign wars, genocide, murder, torture, imprisonment, starvation, destitution, discrimination, unemployment, and the ever-present threat of these and other oppressive measures (Hunt and Sherman 1986; Pope John Paul II 1982; Tucker 1978).

Selected Contemporary Manifestations of Injustice and Oppression

Contemporary manifestations of injustice and oppression within societies, as well as in worldwide relations, are typically experienced, perceived, and challenged as supposedly discrete, unrelated phenomena, such as racism, sexism, ageism, and discrimination by sexual orientation, disabilities, religions, etc. However, in spite of their social, psychological, political, and historical uniqueness, these different manifestations of discrimination appear to have ancient common sources, and they continue to interact, intersect, and overlap. They have all been shaped for centuries by the dynamics and logic of patriarchy, occupational and social caste and class differentiations, ancient and recent slavery, medieval feudalism and colonialism, early and advanced capitalism, chauvinism, economic imperialism, and globalization of production and markets.

Contemporary racism, which refers to oppression, exploitation, and injustice resulting from discriminatory attitudes and practices toward different racial and ethnic groups, derives from the ancient practice of invading the domains of other societies in order to exploit and appropriate their resources and products, and to capture and enslave their people. In spite of important objective and subjective differences, the experiences of Native American peoples, coercively imported slaves from Africa, Hispanic and Asian legal and undocumented immigrants and migrant workers, and Jews and other ethnic groups fleeing poverty, persecution, and pogroms in Europe, reflect the practices and dynamics of economic, social, and psychological domination and exploitation imposed by many societies upon "strangers," ever since the development of agriculture.

Oppression, exploitation, and injustice by social class, on the other hand, which usually intersect and overlap with the dynamics of racism, derive from early processes of occupational, social, and spatial differentiations among fellow citizens within societies, and from subsequently coercively established and maintained, continuously expanding and intensifying inequalities among social groups, concerning resource stewardship, work and production, exchange and distribution, and governance and socialization.

In spite of ideologically shaped illusions in people's consciousness concerning "the blessings of liberty and democracy," contemporary social class structures under advanced capitalism, like social castes before them, involve overtly and subtly enforced domination, exploitation, and injustice with regard to the key institutions of social life. Formal and informal criteria for access to, and promotions within and between, different occupations, and the fact that at the base of the occupational class structure are large numbers of people who participate only marginally in the work and wage system, and who experience severe material deprivations, tend to result in fierce competition among individuals and social groups. This economically induced and politically manipulated competition for work and wages tends to be a major arena for conflicts among individuals and social groups, victimized not only by social class dynamics but also by different types of discrimination. The social class dynamics of the contemporary system of wage labor are, therefore, frequently overlooked, as many people experience them mainly as manifestations of racism, sexism, and other types of discrimination.

Domination of women by men had already occurred among some preagricultural societies and thus predates the emergence of institutionalized oppression and exploitation by race and social class. Such early domination of women evolved in relation to biological aspects of the life process and the organization of work, as childbearing, breastfeeding, and the care of offspring caused real limitations on women's activities. Women seem to have assumed major responsibilities for children early in social evolution, before the role of men in procreation came to be fully understood. Early forms of domination of women, before societies were able to generate a stable economic surplus, and before societal values changed from equality, cooperation, and community toward their opposites, did not, however, involve as severe economic exploitation and injustice as during later stages of social evolution.

While in some preagricultural societies men tended to dominate women, this tendency was by no means universal during that early stage. Rather, many societies revered women as the source of all life. They were presumed to possess superior powers, and were therefore accorded leading social and political responsibilities. This tendency was reflected symbolically in early myths and religions, which assigned central roles to goddesses and female priesthoods (Eisler 1987).

Sexism as we know it today—institutionalized oppression and exploitation of women—emerged following the agricultural revolution, in interaction, with invasions by nomadic, patriarchic peoples, the spread of warfare, the enslavement of conquered societies, the economic and sexual exploitation of captured strangers, and the emergence of occupational and spatial differentiations and social and economic stratifications within societies. All these developments came to be reflected in major value shifts toward inequality, domination, exploitation, competition, and selfishness; in the spreading of patriarchic patterns of social organization; and in corresponding myths, religions, and ideologies.

Sexism evolved gradually into a nearly universal practice. Its manifestations, however, have varied in form and intensity, throughout history among societies and cultures. Moreover, sexism has always interacted with other forms of oppression and exploitation, including race and social class, and it can, therefore, neither be fully understood nor overcome, apart from all other manifestations of domination, exploitation, and injustice.

Discrimination against homosexual men and women seems rooted in ancient fears of behavioral differences and tendencies to oppress strangers and minorities. It also reflects tendencies to enforce conformity with patriarchic patterns of social organization and with patterns of sexual relations compatible with the conservation of patriarchy. Contemporary oppression and injustice toward homosexual men and women, while still rooted in fears of, and resistance to, different and usually repressed sexual tendencies, intersects, and interacts with other dimensions of discrimination that permeate struggles for survival, advantage, and dominance in the competitive context of class structures of advanced capitalism.

Contemporary discrimination against aged persons reflects a recent challenge to, and partial reversal of, early societal tendencies toward domination of younger people by their elders. Like the early domination of women by men, the dominance of older people in early societies was rooted in biological dimensions of the life process and of the organization of work. An objective element of that domination was the wealth of experience—and of knowledge and skills—acquired by the elderly over the course of life. Finally, since life for most people was relatively short then, aged individuals were few in numbers, and were therefore revered. The gradual reversal of the dominant status of the elderly reflects several developments during recent centuries, including:

- a relative decline in knowledge and skills of older people, as younger age groups benefited from an acceleration of innovation in science and technology, disseminated through formal education; and
- a relative decline in the size of the employed work force, in the context of competition for access and promotion, which resulted in delayed entry for the young, and earlier retirement for many among the aged.

A countervailing force to these developments is a relative increase in the size of the aged population as a result of a prolongation of life, and a related increase in their political influence. As a contemporary phenomenon, ageism intersects with other dimensions of discrimination in the prevailing competitive societal context, and cannot be understood and dealt with apart from that context.

Biological, Psychological, and Victim-Blaming Perspectives

So far, my analysis has used social, cultural, economic, and historic-evolutionary perspectives. To complete this sketch of the origin and evolution of injustice and oppression, several further perspectives are noted below, some complementary to, and others in conflict with, the former perspectives.

Freud and other psychoanalysts have posited a biologically based human tendency toward aggression in social and sexual relations, which is expressed in violent and oppressive relations between individuals and social groups. Freud even suggested an inherent death drive (Freud 1959; Fromm 1973; Storr 1968).

Konrad Lorenz and other ethologists who studied animal behavior concluded that aggressive impulses, and struggles for domination and territory, are biologically innate. They drew analogies from observations of animals to humans, in interpreting violence and oppressive relations on individual and social levels (Lorenz 1966).

The biological dimension of human behavior and social relations stressed by psychoanalysis and ethology is an appropriate complement to social, cultural, and historic-evolutionary perspectives on violence, oppression, and injustice. However, one must not infer inevitability from biologically given possibilities. While human capacities for aggression, competition, and violence are supported by massive evidence, so are the capacities for love, care, cooperation, and mutual support. Freud and especially Lorenz, and many of their followers, seem to view biological possibilities apart from social and cultural dynamics rather than in close interaction with them. It is these latter dynamics, however, that influence human choices between biologically possible destructive and constructive tendencies and behaviors.

There seems to be a further fallacy in Lorenz's extrapolation from animal behavior to humans (Montague 1968). Animal behavior is genetically determined to a significantly larger extent than human behavior. As a result of biological evolution, human genetic programs have become less specific and more open, along with gradual increases in the capacities of the human brain. Humans are able to, and must individually and collectively choose specific patterns of life among biologically possible alternatives, since few specific patterns, except for certain reflexes, are imprinted in their genetic makeup. Social designs and their cultural transmission have, therefore, replaced, in the human species, predominantly genetic transmissions of patterns of life of animal species. Accordingly, while humans do have biological capacities to act and relate destructively, and have often chosen to do so, they also have biological capacities to act and relate constructively, have often chosen to do so, and can do so again (Gil 1992).

Psychological perspectives on oppression and injustice tend to consider fear and resentment of strangers, and attitudes of ethnic and class superiority, apart from economic motivations and social-cultural interactions throughout history. Such ahistoric, reductionistic, psychological interpretations tend to fragment oppression and injustice into supposedly discrete types, based on symptoms rather than causes, such as racism, anti-Semitism, sexism, and other discriminatory practices, each to be overcome on its own terms. While symptom-focused psychological analyses, and reform efforts derived from them, are not without merit, their contribution to understanding and overcoming oppression and injustice seems limited.

A final perspective on oppression and social injustice to be noted here reflects a conservative, "victim-blaming" ideology (Ryan 1971). According to this perspective, since civil and political rights have been equalized under law, unjust conditions experienced by individuals and social groups are now due mainly to their own lack of motivation, initiative, and sense of responsibility, and to their allegedly inferior capacities rather than to prevailing oppressive social structures and dynamics. Moreover, neoconservative policy analysts argue that social welfare programs, designed to ease the consequences of oppression and injustice (e.g., Aid to Families with Dependent Children), actually cause intergenerational welfare dependency. Based on such controversial arguments, they suggest abolishing income support programs for people in poverty, and enforcing their exposure to the vagaries and discipline of the labor market (Murray 1984; Cloward and Piven 1992).

Victim-blaming interpretations, too, disregard the history of relations among different social, occupational, and ethnic groups and classes, and the destructive, long-term effects of oppression and injustice on individual and social development. Moreover, these interpretations confuse formal, legal equality with substantive social equality and equality of economic opportunity, and they tend to mistake effects for causes.

3

Social-Change Strategies to Overcome Injustice and Oppression

Some Insights from History

The long history of social change efforts reveals insights into strategies that failed, as well as into strategies that actually worked. Potentially effective strategies can be devised by rejecting the ones that failed, and by developing alternatives that avoid past mistakes.

One important insight gained from the past is that social change activists need to differentiate short-range goals or emergency measures from long-range goals. Each of these is likely to require different strategies, geared to their specific goals and time perspective. This chapter is concerned mainly with long-range social transformation. Transition policies aimed at short-range goals are discussed in chapter 5.

Efforts toward short-range and emergency goals are not only necessary, but are also ethically valid, in order to reduce the intensity of injustice and oppression as fast as possible, even before eliminating its sources in the fabric of societies. However, short-range efforts should not be confused with, and should not substitute for, the pursuit of the long-range goal of fundamental social change, to overcome these destructive conditions at their roots.

Other insights suggested by past liberation struggles concern the

widely held, intuitive view, that coercion and violence are valid strategies toward social justice and liberation from oppression. This controversial issue will be examined later on in this chapter.

Further insights learned from history include:

- that human actions have actually always changed social conditions,
  although people tend to perceive the institutional realities of their
  particular times as more or less constant, and to feel powerless to
  bring about significant changes, even when they feel victimized by
  social conditions;
- that social realities, at any point in time, are results of social change
  efforts and struggles by many people living in earlier times, e.g., the
  transformation of feudalism into early capitalism;
- that in efforts to improve unsatisfactory conditions, people tend to
  pursue individual solutions within a political-economic status quo
  rather than collective solutions in everyone's interest, which would
  require extended efforts to achieve significant social transformations;
- that the relative stability of social orders is maintained not only by
  coercion and control by powerful social elites, but also by the tacit
  consent and cooperation of most people; and
- that people do actually have the potential power to bring about fundamental changes in their social conditions by collective resistance to
  established social orders (Freire 1970; Sharp 1973).

Past social change efforts reveal also that their agents have frequently been movements of committed activists. Members of such
movements are secular missionaries: they agitate among victims of
oppressive and discriminatory practices, and they recruit people to join
their movements in collective, change-oriented efforts. Illustrations of
social change movements from recent history are liberation movements of racial and ethnic minorities, of women, of homosexual people, of "senior citizens," of people with physical, mental, and emotional disabilities, and of "welfare rights" advocates.

The Logic of Overcoming Injustice and Oppression

Prevention theory, derived from public health principles, suggests that
liberation from injustice and oppression requires eradication of their
basic causes in the fabric of societies rather than merely marginal or
liberal modifications of the social status quo. Accordingly, since our

analysis identified coercively established and maintained inequalities concerning the key institutions of social life as the sources of injustice and oppression, establishment of just and nonoppressive societies would require elimination of all systemic inequalities which underlie and reproduce domination and exploitation of some individuals and groups by others.

Furthermore, since the coercive initiation, perpetuation, and intensification of systemic inequalities within and among societies has given rise in people's consciousness to values and ideologies stressing inequality, individualism, selfishness, domination, competition, and disregard for community (from local to global levels), social transformation seems to require shifts in consciousness toward alternative values and ideologies affirming equality, individuality, liberty, cooperation, community and global solidarity.

And finally, since injustice and oppression have been initiated through coercively wrought changes in social institutions and people's consciousness, and are being perpetuated through overt and covert coercive processes, transformation seems to require noncoercive strategies toward changes in consciousness and social institutions, in order to interrupt and reverse the vicious circles of violence.

Long-Range Visions of Just and Nonoppressive Societies

Fundamental social transformations toward just and nonoppressive social orders are unlikely to come about through spontaneous, brief, revolutionary events, nor through "automatic historic processes," or extra-human forces. Rather, they seem to require lengthy processes, involving countercultural education toward critical consciousness, initiated and sustained by social movements, seeking to transform development-inhibiting institutions from local to global levels, into development-conducive alternatives. Such transformation processes, and movements committed to them, require long-range visions to guide them, and to test the compatibility of their strategies with their goals.

Visions of transformation movements need to identify essential attributes of just and nonoppressive social institutions, and their underlying values and philosophies, but need not specify every detail. For visions are not blueprints of every aspect of future societies, but merely sketches of principles of social justice which may be implemented in different ways, by different societies, at different times and places, and at different stages of knowledge and technological development. The visions should reflect, however, the common interest of every individual, social group, and people in meeting their basic human needs, including biological-material, social-psychological, productive-creative, security, self-actualization, and spiritual needs (Gil 1992; Maslow 1970). Accordingly, long-range visions of just, nonoppressive, egalitarian, and truly democratic societies would have to include the following institutional attributes (Gil 1992; Rawls 1971; Tawney 1931; United Nations 1992).

- Natural and human-created productive resources, such as land, water, air, minerals, vegetation, and wildlife; knowledge and technology; schools, libraries, and other cultural facilities; tools and factories; banks and financial institutions; hospitals, clinics, and social services would have to be considered and administered as "public trust," or "commons," available to everyone, on equal terms, for use in productive, life-sustaining, and life-enhancing pursuits.

Stewardship of the public trust, including decisions on priorities of resource allocation, would have to be carried out through decentralized, horizontally coordinated, democratic processes, from local to global levels. While the public trust would replace private and corporate ownership and control of natural and human-created productive resources, consumption goods, such as homes, furnishings, etc., could be owned by individuals and groups of people.

- Work and production would have to be reorganized, redefined, and redesigned, to meet the actual needs for goods and services of all people, anywhere on earth.

Education for, and participation in, work and production, in accordance with individual capacities, would have to be assured to all throughout life. All people would have to have rights, responsibilities, and opportunities to become self-directing "masters of production," who use their mental, physical, and emotional faculties in an integrated manner rather than be forced to labor as "hired hands," or "factors of production," under alienating conditions, in the perceived interest, and at the discretion, of individual or corporate employers.

The ancient, dehumanizing, development-inhibiting division of intellectual work and physical labor would thus be overcome.

Furthermore, all people would have to have equal rights, responsibilities, and constraints, to choose their occupations; to design, direct, and carry out their work; and to share, by rotation, in socially necessary work, not chosen voluntarily by enough people.

Also, work would have to be redefined to include all activities conducive to the maintenance and enrichment of life, and would have to exclude life-impeding activities. Thus, for instance, caring for one's children or dependent relatives would have to be considered and rewarded as socially necessary work, while weapons manufacture—to use an extreme example—might have to be considered "nonwork" or "counterwork," and might have to be phased out. All socially necessary and useful work would have to be deemed to be of equal worth and rewarded accordingly.

Finally, all work would have to be in harmony with nature and with global demographic developments: it would, therefore, have to produce high-quality, long-lasting goods and services, use renewable resources wherever possible, avoid waste of natural and human-generated resources, and would thus be compatible with the requirements of conservation.

- Products of people's work would have to be exchanged and distributed on fair, nonexploitative terms. All people engaging in socially necessary, useful work, regardless of its type, would have to have equal rights to have their needs acknowledged and met, including the needs of their dependent children and other dependent relatives, by obtaining goods and services, adequate in quantity and quality. Also, social, civil, cultural, and political rights and responsibilities would have to be assured to all on equal terms.
- Structures and processes of decision-making and governance, on local and translocal levels, would have to be truly democratic, nonhierarchic, decentralized, horizontally coordinated, and geared to assuring the equal rights and responsibilities, and serving the real needs and interests of everyone living now and in the future. Government service would not entitle elected and appointed officials to privileged living conditions relative to the living conditions of the people whom they represent and serve.
- Socialization practices, during all stages of life, would have to be

shaped by egalitarian and democratic values, so that all children and adults would have equal rights, responsibilities, and opportunities to develop in accordance with their potential, with due regard to individual differences in needs, capacities, and limitations.

When people encounter long-range visions of just and nonoppressive societies, like the one sketched above, they tend to doubt that such visions could actually ever be realized. Such skepticism is understandable, given peoples' lifelong experiences with prevailing social, economic, political, and cultural realities, and their adaptation to, and identification with, these realities.

People who lived long ago would have been similarly skeptical concerning the possibility of ever realizing long-range visions involving comprehensive transformations toward contemporary ways of life. Yet, such transformations did come about, not quickly and spontaneously, but through lengthy processes, involving efforts and struggles by critical thinkers, social activists, and popular movements. By analogy, one may hypothesize, that visions of just and nonoppressive societies, which seem to most people unrealistic and utopian, could eventually be realized through persistent efforts and struggles, over lengthy periods of time, by contemporary and future thinkers, activists, and social movements.

Theoretical Perspectives on Transformation Strategies

Social transformation toward a long-range vision, like the one sketched above, involves discerning, and eventually overcoming, forces and processes which maintain, and continuously reproduce, existing unjust and oppressive societies and their cultures.

Human societies and their particular institutional systems have always been shaped and reshaped by the actions and social relations, and by the consciousness of their members. Hence, the forces and processes which liberation movements have to target for transformation include:

- patterns of actions, interactions, and social relations of the members of societies, and
- processes of consciousness which underlie, motivate, and facilitate the existing patterns of actions, interactions, and social relations.

Transformation of unjust and oppressive societies into just and nonoppressive ones would require major changes in patterns of people's actions, interactions, and social relations. In turn, such changes seem to depend on changes of people's consciousness, which would be conducive to alternative patterns of actions and relations. Activists, pursuing long-range visions of social justice, ought, therefore, to devise and implement strategies aimed at facilitating the emergence of "critical consciousness," in order to induce and sustain appropriate changes in people's actions, interactions, and social relations (Freire 1970; 1973). Having identified consciousness as a force for maintaining and reproducing unjust and oppressive social orders, as well as a potential force for transforming such orders into just and nonoppressive ones by spreading critical consciousness, the nature and dynamics of human consciousness ought to be examined before discussing strategies for social transformation.

Nature and Dynamics of Consciousness

Consciousness is a mental faculty by which people become aware of, and can reflect about, themselves, their natural and social environment, and relations between themselves and the environment. Consciousness emerges from active engagement with one's world rather than from passive absorption of it. It involves internalization of a particular "socially constructed reality," adaptation to it, and integration into it, as well as reflection about and imagining alternatives to this reality as a basis for reconstructing it.

People tend to form in their consciousness images of their societies' concrete ways of life as a result of experiencing, observing, and actively participating in, these ways of life. Social scientists tend to refer to these images in people's consciousness as "symbolic universe" (Berger and Luckman 1966; Gil 1992).

Internalization into consciousness of aspects of one's social position, social class, and entire society, enables people to think, act, and relate in accordance with societal norms and expectations. As they do so, guided by their consciousness, their behavior, in turn, reinforces their consciousness of the prevailing symbolic universe, and their capacity to participate appropriately in the concrete ways of life. In short, participation in established ways of life shapes one's consciousness of them, which facilitates further participation and reinforcement of consciousness—a lifelong process of interaction of behavior and consciousness.

The symbolic universe that individuals form in their consciousness reflects reality as constructed by a particular society in the course of its unique history. It does not reflect "objective" reality, which is probably unknowable, as all knowledge emerges through societal processes, and is affected by them. The versions of the symbolic universe in the consciousness of different individuals in the same society tend to vary. People, especially in complex, internally divided societies, differ in social conditions and social class position, as well as in individual history, biology, and characteristics. All these dimensions affect the emergence of individual consciousness. As a result, the consciousness of different individuals in the same society will overlap, but will also differ. People's ability to communicate and interact effectively will be affected by the extent of overlap and difference in their individual consciousness. The consciousness and symbolic universe of people from different groups and classes within a society, and from different societies, may differ markedly. These differences can cause difficulties in communications and interactions.

Failure to develop a symbolic universe in one's consciousness that corresponds roughly with that of people with whom one lives—the cause of the failure may be organic, social, psychological, or political-philosophical—may interfere with an individual's ability to function in social situations and relations. Such individuals may be considered "deviant" or "insane," when their behavior does not conform to what is considered normal in their society, but reflects a unique, individual consciousness and symbolic universe.

The consciousness of people reflects their subjective perceptions of socially constructed reality, and serves as a frame of reference for individual thoughts and actions in everyday life. In accordance with the internal logic of individual consciousness, human behavior is always "rational," i.e., oriented toward the subjective goals of individual actors, and makes sense to them at the time they engage in it, given their perceptions and feelings. Subjectively rational behavior may, however, seem irrational to others whose consciousness, perceptions and frames of reference differ from the individuals whose behavior they observe. It may also seem irrational to the individuals themselves, when their perceptions, feelings, and frames of reference change with time. For "rational" behavior is always relative to a content-and-time-specific consciousness.

The above discussion suggests that social life proceeds simultaneously on two interacting and interdependent levels, neither of which can function without the other: the level of concrete behavior, and that of consciousness, of individual members of society. People cannot act unless their consciousness is engaged in their actions, and their actions are prefigured in their consciousness. For action and thought, or body and mind, are usually a living unity rather than separate domains.

Consciousness serves usually as a medium for individual adaptation to established ways of life, and hence as a force for societal continuity. However, it can also evolve into "critical consciousness," and serve as a medium for critical reflection, and as a source for innovation of ways of life, based on alternative perceptions of needs and interests. Such transformations of consciousness can be communicated to others, and can lead to collective actions aimed at social and cultural transformations.

The capacities of people for critical consciousness and for initiating social change are not actualized easily, however. Major obstacles to their actualization are that critical consciousness can emerge only gradually as children mature, but that the critical use of consciousness is usually not encouraged in the course of socialization. Critical consciousness is least developed during infancy and childhood—crucial stages of socialization during which children experience strong pressures for adaptation to established ways of life. Moreover, socialization of children occurs under conditions of physical, emotional, social, and economic dependence on adults who dispense rewards and sanctions, and are perceived as all-powerful. These circumstances reduce opportunities for the emergence of critical consciousness, and enhance opportunities for consciousness to serve societal continuity. They are, therefore, important sources of the prevalence of conservative tendencies in social evolution, rooted, as they are, in the societal dynamics and biological aspects of the relationship of children and adults.

One further aspect of consciousness which strengthens conservative tendencies is that children experience and come to perceive established ways of life as "objective reality," to be taken for granted as valid and permanent—a force demanding submission and resisting challenge. The human origin of prevailing ways of life is thus obscured, and gods, heroes, and superhuman ancestors are credited with "having created" them. Having developed such a consciousness of socially constructed reality while growing up, people are poorly prepared to critically examine established institutional systems, and to become involved in movements for comprehensive social change, even when their basic needs cannot be met. Instead, they tend to view particular problems that affect them as isolated fragments, and to seek issue-specific, incremental solutions, which leave established ways of life essentially unchanged.

Themes of Consciousness Relevant to Social Change

Several themes relevant to strategies for social change can usually be discerned in the consciousness of individuals and in the symbolic universe of societies. It should be noted that, though these themes can be distinguished conceptually from one another, as is done in the following discussion, they are interacting dimensions of unified mental processes:

Images of established ways of life: These images are the abstract equivalent of the concrete aspects of social life, its institutions, customs and traditions, and the prevailing circumstances of living of people, their relative social power, and their social relations. They serve as a road map of the social landscape in which people are expected to move, act, and relate. Without such a map, people would feel disoriented and incapable of appropriate involvement in their society.

Systems of ideas and beliefs: This theme involves interpretations of nature, human nature, and the universe; life and death; origin and destination; time and space; the known, unknown, and unknowable; relations among these notions, and their relation to the concrete ways of life of a society. It is a depository of "common sense" or "conventional wisdom," and of assumptions concerning essentially incomprehensible phenomena that humans confront, and which they interpret and reinterpret, motivated by their "spiritual needs."

Perceptions of individual and collective needs and interests: These perceptions are the sources of the internal logic and rationality of ways of life, and of the motivations, attitudes, values, and behaviors of individuals. The core of this theme is awareness of biologically rooted, basic human needs, and of corresponding, real human interest in the fulfillment of these needs. However, perceptions of socially defined needs, and of corresponding human interests in fulfillment of these socially shaped needs, tend to be superimposed upon this awareness. Depending on the scope and intensity of these superimposed perceptions, the actual awareness of basic needs and interests may be displaced from consciousness into the subconscious and unconscious (Freud 1938). Such changes in awareness and perceptions result from socialization in internally divided societies, when dominant classes, by virtue of their hegemony over systems of ideas are able to induce most people to perceive their needs and interests in ways compatible with the perceived needs and interests of social elites (Hoare and Smith 1971).

An illustration of displacement from consciousness of basic needs and real interests by socially superimposed ones is the pursuit of material wealth, perceived as a source of fulfillment of all one's needs. Success in accumulating wealth may, however, not assure fulfillment of the basic need for meaningful human relations.

In addition to awareness of basic and socially shaped needs and interests, this theme involves also awareness of individual motivation to act in ways perceived as conducive to fulfillment of these needs.

Finally, this theme of consciousness involves also the vague notion of "collective needs and interests," which can be illustrated by concepts such as "national interest" and "national security." These concepts have a strong emotional appeal which tends to inhibit reflection and reasoned analysis of their actual meaning. Collective needs and interests refer, undoubtedly, to individual needs and interests shared by some collectivity. What is usually not specified, however, is who belongs to that collectivity. In subtle ways, the impression is conveyed that the needs and interests of every member of society are included.

In small, classless societies, the needs and interests of every member may indeed be included in, and represented by, collective needs and interests. However, in large societies, divided internally into social classes, "collective needs and interests" are usually defined by dominant classes in accordance with their perceived needs and interests.

Yet, the emotional appeal of terms such as "national interests" and "national security" tends to mobilize support from dominated classes for policies and actions which are potentially damaging to their real needs and interests. Many wars, fought mainly in the interest of social elites of large, divided societies, illustrate the readiness of dominated classes to serve, suffer, and die for a "national interest" which may not include their individual needs and interests.

Social values and personal values: Values are guidelines which people developed in the course of societal evolution, to differentiate behaviors whose outcomes they "valued," and which they, therefore, considered proper and worthy of repetition, from behaviors whose outcomes they disliked and did "not value," and which they, therefore, considered improper and not worthy of repetition. In other words, values are behavioral rules to distinguish "good" actions from "evil" ones, and to ensure repetition of "good" actions, and avoidance of "evil" ones.

The yardstick or frame of reference for what is "good" and "valued," and what is "evil" and "not valued," are the real and perceived needs and interests of those who judge or "evaluate" behaviors. Accordingly, values are always rooted in real and perceived needs and interests. Behind every social value, one can, therefore, discern certain interests, and value analysis should always explore whose interests are to be served by given values. Social values can represent everyone's needs and interests, such as respect for and preservation of everyone's life and well-being, or represent only the needs and interests of particular social groups or classes, such as preservation of privileged conditions for aristocrats, owners of property, males, and members of the white race.

In the course of history, dominant social groups succeeded in coercing and inducing dominated groups to internalize and accept as valid those social values which served the perceived needs and interests of the dominant groups, but affected adversely the needs and interests of dominated groups. Women have internalized values assuring male privilege, and propertyless classes and the common people have internalized values assuring the sanctity of property and the privileged conditions of aristocrats. Even members of nonwhite races have, at times, internalized values assuring the privileged conditions of white people.

The internalization of social values serving the perceived needs and interests of dominant social groups seems to have been achieved initially through coercive measures. However, coercion was gradually complemented, and often replaced, by processes of socialization and social control rooted in, and aided by, mythology, organized religion, and ideology. These systems of ideas, which were developed by priesthoods and cultural elites, associated usually with dominant social classes, denied the human origin of values, and projected their origin onto gods and spirits, whom they endowed with imaginary powers to inflict severe sanctions for nonsubmission to established social values (e.g., damnation to hell).

While organized religions have usually supported and disseminated values representing the needs and interests of dominant social classes, the sources of religions and their "prophetic" traditions reflect values which represent the real needs and interests of all people. Prophets, in opposition to priesthoods, usually advocated social justice, equality of all people, love, and mutualism, and they called for establishment of just social orders "here and now" rather than in an "afterlife" or a "kingdom of heaven." The Bible—the books of the prophets, the Gospels—and the Koran, as well as sacred scriptures of other religions, provide ample evidence for the roots of religions in the yearnings of people for social justice, equality, and liberation from oppression. "Liberation Theology" is a contemporary expression of this strong countercurrent to organized religion (Gutierrez 1973).

Dominated social classes who submit to, and accept the validity of, social values which adversely affect their needs and interests, while serving the perceived needs and interests of dominant classes, are usually larger in numbers than the latter. By virtue of their numbers, they have potential power to transform social institutions in ways conducive to the satisfaction of their needs and interests. However, they are unlikely to act together toward fundamental changes of ways of life in accordance with their needs and interests unless they reject in their consciousness the validity of social values which uphold the privileged conditions of dominant social classes (Sharp 1973).

While most people will usually internalize into their consciousness the dominant values of their society, there are nevertheless also sets of "personal" values in everyone's consciousness, which may differ from overtly professed values, and which may influence their behavior in everyday life. When personal values are in conflict with accepted social values, contradictions are likely to become manifest in people's behaviors. The prevalence of antisocial and criminal behavior, as well as acts of civil disobedience and conscientious objection, all of which do not conform to dominant social values, illustrate this possibility.

When planning strategies to overcome injustice and oppression, one needs to be concerned mainly with value dimensions which influence the key institutions of social life. These value dimensions include:

- equality vs. inequality
- liberty vs. domination and exploitation
- individuality vs. selfishness and individualism
- life-affirmation vs. disregard for life
- collectivity-orientation vs. disregard for community
- cooperation vs. competition.

The ways of life of societies tend to reflect the positions of most of its people on these interrelated value dimensions. For the value positions of majorities in societies will, invariably, influence the development of social policies, and will constrain the range of possible changes in the social status quo. Fundamental social transformations are, therefore, unlikely to occur unless they are preceded by significant shifts in the consciousness of many people of a society with regard to these value dimensions.

Ideologies: According to a dictionary of sociology, an ideology is

a system of interdependent ideas (beliefs, traditions, principles, and myth) held by a social group or society, which reflects, rationalizes, and defends its particular social, moral, religious, political, and economic institutional interests and commitments. Ideologies serve as logical and philosophical justifications for a group's patterns of behavior, as well as its attitudes, goals, and general life situation. The ideology of any population involves an interpretation (and usually a repudiation) of alternative ideological frames of reference. The elements of an ideology tend to be accepted as truth or dogma rather than as tentative philosophical and theoretical formulations, despite the fact that ideologies are modified in accordance with sociocultural changes.

(Theodorson and Theodorson 1969)

Ideologies are products of human actions and thoughts throughout social evolution. They interpreted, justified, and reinforced ways of life as they emerged and were reproduced and stabilized, regardless of differences in institutional orders. Ideologies thus became a force assuring relative stability of any social order, and came to reflect the interests of individuals and classes who supported a status quo from which they benefited, objectively and subjectively.

With the passage of time, as societies grew in size and became fragmented into dominant and dominated classes, and as institutional patterns and ideological systems became more complex, the origins of the institutions and ideologies in collective human actions and reflections were gradually forgotten. Along with this collective amnesia, extrahuman forces, in the form of human-created gods, came to be perceived as creators of life and originators of social institutions and ideologies. This projection from humans unto infallible, almighty, superhuman agents greatly enhanced the influence of ideologies over the everyday behavior and consciousness of people. For, henceforth, to question ideological premises involved a challenge to the gods and their absolute truth and power. Social sanctions for such challenges were usually swift and extreme. These projections and sanctions were certainly compatible with the perceived interests of dominant social classes, whose very dominance and privileged circumstances were justified and legitimated by prevailing ideologies.

As the ways of life which ideologies reflect underwent evolutionary and, at times, revolutionary transformations in the course of history, so did ideologies. However, in spite of constant interactions between institutional patterns and ideologies, the correspondence between these concrete and abstract dimensions of social life is usually not a perfect one. Rather, there are often time lags between changes in practice and changes in ideologies, and there are also contradictions between them, so much so that some students of society have viewed these dimensions as separate domains: the world of action and human relations, and the world of ideas.

The more complex and fragmented societies became in the course of change and development, the more difficult became the task of creating illusions of inclusive societal interests, and the less successful became the process of ideological integration and indoctrination. Real and perceived conflicts of interests among age groups, sexes, families, clans, tribes, races, religions, castes, and social classes within politically unified societies gave rise to variations on ideological themes, to internal contradictions, and to emergence of counter ideologies.

Dominant, privileged social classes have usually held hegemonic roles in the development and dissemination of ideologies. Most people tend, therefore, to internalize ideologies which are disseminated by, and compatible with the interest of, social elites, but potentially damaging to their own real interests. Unless people encounter and internalize alternative ideologies, reflective of their own needs and interests, or somehow develop such alternative ideologies together with others with whom they share life experiences and social conditions, they are likely to support in consciousness and actions, ways of life and policies which inhibit their development and well-being.

Critical consciousness: This aspect of consciousness inheres in the human capacity for critical reflection. It is the Achilles' heel of all established social orders, and a necessary, though not sufficient, precursor of all social change. Critical consciousness can initiate counterthemes to each major theme of consciousness. It can question and challenge internalized images of established ways of life, their institutional systems and consequences, and their customs and traditions. It can reflect on, and transcend conventional wisdom and common sense, and assumptions concerning nature, human nature, and the universe. It can distinguish between real human needs and interests, and socially shaped, perceived needs and interests. It can unravel values reflective of interests of dominant classes from values reflective of real human needs and interests. And it can generate alternative ideologies and visions of ways of life conducive to the unfolding and actualization of everyone's innate potential, and to the emergence of institutional orders based on social justice and social equality, freedom and genuine democracy, and the affirmation of human life in harmony with nature.

Critical Consciousness: Key to Fundamental Social Change

The analysis of consciousness, and of themes of consciousness relevant to social change, provides important clues for strategies toward the realization of long-range visions of just and nonoppressive societies. To advance such visions by noncoercive, voluntary, truly democratic means (the only strategic mode likely to be effective) rather than by coercive, authoritarian, nondemocratic ones, seems to require transformation of the status quo-reproducing consciousness of most people, into alternative, status quo-challenging critical consciousness.

Were critical consciousness to spread widely among significant majorities of people, from local to global levels, humankind could eliminate prevailing conditions of injustice and oppression. However, critical consciousness is unlikely to expand spontaneously, as its spread tends to be inhibited by biological, social, psychological, cultural, economic, and political realities. Accordingly, social movements, which have come to realize that critical consciousness, and actions based on it, may, indeed, be the key to a meaningful future for the human species, would have to make intense efforts to facilitate its spreading in spite of obstacles. These efforts would involve dialogical, educational processes to promote changes in consciousness, concerning:

- the images of social reality, most people now hold;
- the ideas, beliefs, and assumptions people tend to take for granted, without critical examination;
- the perceptions of individual and collective needs and interests, which underlie and motivate the actions, thoughts, and social relations of most people; and
- the values and ideologies, which derive from the perceptions of needs and interests, and affect the choices, actions, thoughts, and social relations of individuals, social groups, and classes.

As for changes necessary in the images of social reality, people have to be helped to discover that these realities originated in, and are always results of, particular human actions, thoughts, and social relations; that people have changed these realities in the past and will change them again in the future; and that people, by acting together, do have power to influence the directions of future changes, even though, as isolated individuals, they feel, and are, powerless to do so.

People also have to be helped to realize that prevailing conditions of multidimensional social inequalities were established, and are being reproduced, by overt and covert coercion and socialization rather than by "acts of gods," or by voluntary, democratic choices. And finally, people would have to realize, that "law and order" in the context of "legitimate" social inequalities, does not imply justice and freedom from oppression, for the existing legal system tends, actually, to uphold injustice and oppression.

Ideas, beliefs, and assumptions that people have to be helped to examine and transcend include the mistaken views that humans are compelled, rather than merely enabled, by nature, to be selfish, greedy, competitive, and violent; and that, therefore, just, nonoppressive, egalitarian, cooperative, and nonviolent societies have never existed, nor is it possible to establish such societies now, or in the future (Kropotkin 1956).

People would also have to examine whether human nature corresponds to dominant assumptions concerning it. This would enable them to unravel the "social" and "individual" dimensions of the human species, interactions between these dimensions, and possible tensions between them. The source of the social dimension is the inability of infants to survive and become fully human without care by adults and socialization in a community and culture. The source of the individual dimension is the uniqueness of every person in genetic, social, historical, experiential, and psychological terms. Once people come to understand these intrinsic aspects of the human condition, they are likely to realize that individuality can develop optimally only in the context of vital communities, but fails to develop adequately in the context of individualistic pursuits, unrelated to, or damaging to, a community (Fromm 1955; NCCB 1986).

Other widely held beliefs to be examined and challenged are that everyone who really tries can secure satisfactory living conditions by working hard within the established social order, in spite of prevailing unjust and oppressive social realities; that, therefore, no major structural changes, but only marginal adjustments, may be necessary in the societal status quo; and that people who fail to secure adequate conditions may be inherently deficient, and would have to blame themselves for not having tried hard enough; such people would simply have to change their attitudes and practices and try harder (Ryan 1971). Furthermore, people ought to examine Adam Smith's controversial, yet influential, set of assumptions (which have not been supported by history), that the public good tends to appear spontaneously, as if created and propelled by an "invisible hand," when individuals act selfishly and competitively in pursuit of material gain; and that, therefore, governments should not interfere with supposedly "free markets," nor should they plan for, and attempt to promote, the public good (Smith 1961).

As for changes necessary in the perceptions of individual and collective needs and interests, people have to be helped to realize that the realities of institutionalized inequalities are incompatible with their true interest to satisfy their basic human needs. Given the dynamics of contemporary capitalist societies and cultures, many people may be able to satisfy their needs for biological-material necessities, though often under alienating and stigmatizing conditions, and at substandard levels. However, given these dynamics, people are usually unable to meet their social-psychological, productive-creative, security, self-actualization, and spiritual needs at adequate levels (Gil 1992; Maslow 1970). The consistent frustration of human needs due to the dynamics of injustice and oppression of contemporary societies is a constant source of social, emotional, and physical pathology and violence, and of individual and community underdevelopment. Confronting these outcomes of prevailing ways of life, for themselves and for their communities, could induce people to revise their perceptions of their needs and interests rather than uphold definitions of interests, and perceptions of needs which reproduce a societal context that leads, inevitably, to continued frustration of their real human needs and inhibits their development.

It is important to note that being "successful" in economic terms, under prevailing social and cultural conditions, does not imply that one's nonmaterial needs are being realized adequately, and that one's development is not inhibited. Affluent people are now as unlikely as poor people to fulfill their social-psychological, productive-creative, security, self-actualization, and spiritual needs. They, too, would, therefore, have to reexamine the current perceptions of their needs and interests, and they, too, might discover that they would be more likely to meet their real needs in a just and nonoppressive society shaped by different perceptions of individual and collective needs and interests.

Finally, people would have to be helped to reexamine the dominant values and ideologies of their society and culture, which they internalized into their consciousness, while growing up and interacting with, and relating to, others in everyday life. Currently dominant values and ideologies evolved along with, and reflect, the established unjust and oppressive social order. Once people internalize these values and ideologies, they come to perceive their interests in adapting to the practices and expectations of their society and they are motivated to think and act in ways which continuously reproduce the institutional status quo.

When people are helped to discover that their real needs are being frustrated consistently in the context of established unjust and oppressive institutions, they are also likely to realize that transforming these institutions into just and nonoppressive alternatives would serve their interest, as it would be conducive to their personal development by enabling them to meet their real needs. These insights would enable them also to recognize the necessity of shifting currently dominant values and ideologies, which sustain unjust and oppressive ways of life, toward alternative values and ideologies, which affirm equality, liberty, individuality, community, cooperation, and harmony with nature.

Strategies to Expand Critical Consciousness

If, as suggested above, transforming unjust and oppressive societies, by democratic means, into just and nonoppressive alternatives, depends on the spreading of critical consciousness, social movements would have to use different, suitable strategies and opportunities to facilitate its spreading. The history of social activism reveals that movements have always pursued consciousness-expanding strategies, including workplace and community struggles, electoral politics, experiments involving living and working cooperatively, and organizing for peace and justice, for liberation of minorities, women, and other groups victimized by discrimination, for environmental protection, and for many other causes. While most of these efforts aimed to expand consciousness focused on specific issues, some did trace the connections of single issues to the dynamics of injustice and oppression, and attempted to spread critical consciousness focused on radical social transformation.

Everyday Life Encounters

Expanding critical consciousness through everyday life encounters involves initiating political discourse in everyday human encounters, at social gatherings and in places of work. It does not negate other strategies, but is meant to enhance them, by using readily available, yet usually overlooked, opportunities for promoting critical consciousness and building social movements.

Whenever people interact in everyday life, their actions and communications can either conform to, or challenge, the social status quo and prevailing patterns of human relations. When people speak and act within the range of "normal" expected behavior, they reinforce the existing social order and its "common-sense" consciousness. On the other hand, when people's words and deeds transcend "normal" behavioral ranges by questioning and challenging the status quo, they create opportunities for the emergence of reflection and critical consciousness on the part of others with whom they interact.

Based on these considerations, the strategy suggested here involves efforts by social activists to "deviate" in everyday encounters from system-reinforcing behaviors, to pose challenging questions, and to engage people in reflection and dialogue concerning consequences of prevailing social, economic, political, and cultural realities for the quality of their life. An apt illustration of this strategy would be to respond to the conventional greeting at social gatherings, "How are you," with the unexpected question, "Do you really want to know? If so, let us talk about how I, you, and everyone else is doing. This is an important issue, people should talk about . . ." It is interesting to note here, how, in our culture, an essentially political question has been depoliticized and transformed into a ritual greeting, to which people do not expect a real reply.

As dialogues evolve, stimulated by the behavior and questions of activists, they could identify themselves as advocates of social and economic justice and real democracy—feasible alternatives to capitalism and plutocracy. They must not practice self-censorship concerning their political perspectives, as people tend to do in unjust and oppressive realities. One cannot help others to extricate themselves from the dominant ideology and culture unless one is comfortable to acknowledge one's alternative political perspective.

When pursuing this proposed strategy, activists need to be sensitive to the thoughts, feelings, and circumstances of people whom they are trying to engage in dialogue. As the goal of these encounters is to stimulate critical reflection, one needs to be sure that people are ready to communicate. Challenging questions are not to be posed for their own sake, but for the sake of initiating a process of dialogue and reflection. Activists will, therefore, have to develop sensitivity to people's readiness, and skills in facilitating dialogue.

Activists initiating political dialogues will also have to be tolerant of positions they reject. For, whatever positions people hold, do make sense to them in terms of their life experiences, circumstances, and frames of reference. People have to be respected in these encounters, even when their positions and values conflict with those of the activists. Activists would also have to avoid presenting their solutions to problems people experience, but would have to help them to evolve their own solutions.

There are many opportunities to act in accordance with this strategy in places of work, and in social situations. Were many activists to use these opportunities routinely, many people might become involved in political discussions, and the taboo against discourse that challenges capitalism might be overcome. Gradually, growing numbers of people might undergo transformations of consciousness, might join transformation movements, and might carry on this strategy.

The only limits on the strategy proposed here are limits of people's energy and commitment, and their levels of comfort when challenging assumptions, values, and practices which tend to be taken for granted by nearly everyone else. Activists need not try to do too much, too soon, but need to develop their skills and sensitivity gradually, in order to avoid "burnout." People using this strategy are likely to benefit by joining support-and-study groups whose members can help one another to examine and improve their political practice.

Professional Practice

The consciousness-expanding strategy suggested above for human encounters in everyday life, can also be integrated into the professional practice of social workers, teachers, physicians, lawyers, ministers, and others whose line of work involves mainly communication with people. When adopting a "radical" approach in their practice, professionals oriented to social change can reduce their own sense of alienation due to the contradictions between their system-transforming perspective and the system-maintaining mission of the organizations and services for which they work. The integration of this political strategy into professional practice is illustrated here briefly with reference to social work and teaching. Radical social work practice is discussed more fully in chapter 6.

Social workers talk with people about difficulties in their lives, their unfulfilled needs, fears, and insecurities, and what one can do about these difficulties. Many social workers discuss these issues as having mainly individual causes, to be overcome by personal adjustment to supposedly unchangeable realities. Radical social workers discuss the same issues as related to dehumanizing social, economic, and political institutions, established by past and present human actions, which humans can change, and adjust to their real needs, by collective actions. Teachers, regardless of their discipline and the ages of their students, and regardless of the orientation of their schools, could teach in imaginative ways, to facilitate exploration of actual realities of prevailing ways of life, their destructive consequences for everyone, everywhere, and feasible approaches toward constructive alternatives.

When using the approach sketched here, radical professionals are likely to encounter conflicts with administrators at their places of work. Peer support groups and labor unions can assist activists to deal constructively with such conflicts, and to defend their civil and political rights to academic and professional freedom. The likelihood of conflicts can often be reduced by testing the limits of what is possible in given work settings, and staying within them. This does not mean compromising one's political perspective. It merely means pursuing this strategy in ways that do not result in dismissal from one's workplace, for nothing is gained by being forced from an arena of political activism. Moreover, upon testing limits, one often discovers that they are actually less severe than one assumed, and that many activists function at a self-imposed, safe distance from actual limits.

Redefining and redesigning social work practice, teaching, and other professions along the lines sketched here involves risks, and requires collective study, reflection, and experimentation, as well as opportunities for support and advice from like-minded colleagues in nonthreatening, horizontal relationships. While implementing such a strategy is difficult, given existing cultural realities, it has real potential for reach-

ing many people, and for spreading critical consciousness on a growing scale. It also can be rewarding for activist professionals, by enabling
them to reclaim their integrity, and by providing an opportunity to pursue their political goals as an integral dimension of their work.

Implicit in the strategy suggested here, whether pursued in human
encounters in everyday life or in professional practice, is the transformation of political activism from special times, occasions, and projects, outside people's regular social and occupational life, into a constant dimension of daily life and work. Should growing numbers of
activists and radical professionals adopt this strategy in addition to, or
even in place of, other political work, the aggregate of social activism,
promoting expansion of critical consciousness, is likely to increase significantly.

Conventional Politics

Conventional politics concerning workplace and community issues,
the rights of groups subjected to discrimination, protection of the environment, electoral politics, etc., tend to pursue short-term goals rather
than long-range visions of fundamental social change. However, radical activists who participate in conventional political efforts have
opportunities to help people trace connections between apparently
separate issues, and discern their common roots in the prevailing social
order. When exposed to such insights, people may realize that they
would have to confront these root causes, in order to deal effectively
with the separate problems they intend to solve. An apt illustration of
this strategy is helping people, aiming to prevent violence and crime,
to discover links between these social ills and poverty, unemployment,
and worker alienation in capitalist societies (Brenner 1984; Gil 1996).

Expanding people's consciousness concerning the interconnections
and the common roots of discrete problems, around which interest
groups tend now to form, could enable them to overcome fragmentation and competition for limited resources. Such fragmentation and
competition are politically dysfunctional, for they reinforce the status
quo of power by reducing the potential collective strength of separate
interest groups. The goal of radical activists in these situations is,
therefore, to transform conventional interest group politics into politics of common human needs.

Advocating values, policies, and programs, compatible with the needs of all people, is expected to enable separate interest groups to unite and form inclusive social change movements. An illustration of the suggested shift from conventional interest group politics toward politics of common human needs, would be a demand for universal rights to, and responsibilities for, useful work and adequate income, in place of demands for "affirmative action," to include formerly excluded and discriminated-against social groups in the existing competitive work system.

Politics of common human needs could also be integrated into electoral politics. Candidates for political office, pursuing visions of a just society and using strategies of spreading critical consciousness, would have to campaign against the systemic roots of social problems rather than against symptoms affecting specific groups. They would also have to advocate policies to meet the human needs of all people rather than specific needs of separate social groups.

Beyond Critical Consciousness: Changing Behavior and Institutions

Societies became what they are through the actions, relations, and consciousness of their members, and they are reproduced through people's socialization and conformity to previously institutionalized patterns of actions, relations, and consciousness. As suggested above, social movements can initiate social change by facilitating the spreading of critical consciousness. But unless shifts in consciousness cause individuals and groups to evolve new patterns of actions and social relations, the process of social change would be stalled on the level of ideas. New patterns of actions and social relations depend on self-transformation by individuals and social groups, as well as on institutional transformations carried out collectively by individuals, groups, and networks among them.

Individual Changes

Changes in the consciousness of individuals concerning social, economic, and political realities, perceptions of individual and collective needs and interests, and social and individual values and ideologies, could gradually lead to changes in attitudes and relations toward people with whom they live and work, as well as toward people elsewhere on earth, and toward the natural environment on which all life depends. People could try to avoid dominating, exploiting, and competing in relation to others, and to reduce socially structured inequalities, and benefits derived from racism, sexism, and other types of discrimination. In their everyday social relations, people could foster cooperation, solidarity, and community, as far as this is possible, in spite of prevailing social structures and dynamics.

People could modify their actions and social relations in accordance with their transformed consciousness, by testing and expanding accepted limits, in settings and situations over which they exercise some influence. They could create in this way "liberated spaces," prefiguring alternative possible futures. People could also reduce their personal involvement in wasteful and destructive consumption of the earth's limited resources, and they could aim to adjust personal life styles to principles of global distributive justice and environmental sustainability. Through such socially less unjust and ecologically less damaging practices, guided by the notion, "act locally and think globally," people could reduce somewhat the contradictions between their newly evolving values and everyday realities (SLC, AFSC 1977).

Collective Changes

The unjust and oppressive institutions and culture of feudalism were transformed gradually into incipient capitalism by small-scale economic activities of individual entrepreneurs and craft guilds in medieval towns, and by the simultaneous spread of humanistic-individualistic philosophical and ideological systems (Hunt and Sherman 1981). Analogously, the transformation of the institutions and culture of the unjust and oppressive global system of mature capitalism could be furthered by the gradual emergence of alternative economic practices that transcend the principles of capitalism, and by the simultaneous spread of emancipatory philosophical and ideological systems, such as democratic socialism.

A renaissance of cooperative economic enterprises began in the eighteenth and nineteenth centuries, and has become a worldwide phenomenon during the twentieth century (Thompson 1994). Cooperative social and economic institutions were the dominant model during preagricultural, nomadic stages of social evolution. In many parts of the world these cooperative institutions survived throughout agricultural stages, and also beyond colonization by European nations (Eisler 1987; Farb 1968; Kropotkin 1956).

Modern cooperative institutions include consumer cooperatives; cooperative financial services such as credit unions, cooperative banks, and rotating community loan funds; producer cooperatives and networks of producer cooperatives for bartering and marketing; and "total" cooperatives which combine cooperative production and consumption with living cooperatively (Blum 1982; Buber 1958; Gil 1979; Lindenfeld and Rothschild-Whitt 1982; Morrison 1991).

Consumer cooperatives are not as significant a challenge to capitalism, as producer cooperatives and total cooperatives. Their major purpose is to reduce the costs of consumption for their members by using their collective purchasing power in markets, and by eliminating the profit factor on the retail level. However, consumer cooperatives demonstrate the value and ideology of cooperation, and in this way they challenge the dominant, competitive ideology of the culture of capitalism.

Producer cooperatives and their marketing associations in the United States and in other countries challenge a basic capitalist principle: the separation of ownership and control of enterprises from workers employed by them to produce goods and services for profitable sales in markets. In producer cooperatives, workers own the means, skills, and knowledge of production, and they control and design the processes of production and the marketing of the goods and services created by their enterprises. While capitalism exists, producer cooperatives are forced to function as capitalist units, responsive to the dynamics of capitalist markets. However, internally they are a cooperative alternative to the dominant competitive economic model. Their spread in many parts of the world, including the United States, could, in theory, replace capitalism gradually from within, in the same way feudalism was gradually transformed. In spite of many difficulties, developing and spreading worker-owned and worker-managed enterprises is a significant action strategy toward a just and nonoppressive economy, society, and culture.

Total collectives, like the kibbutz and kibbutz networks in Palestine and Israel, religious and secular communes in the United States, and communities belonging to the Federation of Egalitarian Communities in the United States, Canada, and Mexico, transcend and challenge capitalism not only as an economic system, but also in social, political, cultural, and philosophical-ideological terms. They are models prefiguring alternative just and nonoppressive societies, and they demonstrate the feasibility of creating such comprehensive alternatives within prevailing realities. They also reveal the difficulties involved in creating such alternatives. Yet, like producer cooperatives, they are important elements of a comprehensive strategy for social transformation, for they combine into a living reality the transformation of consciousness, actions, and social relations (Buber 1958; Gil 1979; Kanter 1972 1973; FIC and CPC 1990; Spiro 1970).

Violence and Social Change

It is widely assumed that violence and "armed struggle" are necessary to overcome injustice and oppression. It is, therefore, important to examine this assumption when developing strategies for human liberation.

Since the concept of violence lacks a generally accepted definition, its meaning needs to be clarified for purposes of this discussion. Manifestations of violence are frequently perceived, and dealt with, as discrete events. Analysis suggests, however, that such supposedly discrete events are actually moments of historical, multidimensional (social, economic, political, cultural, and psychological) processes, from local to global levels. More specifically, they seem to be moments in gradually intensifying vicious circles, involving the following interacting phases:

- *initiating societal violence* within and among human groups, i.e., domination of some individuals and social groups by others, to exploit them socially and economically;
- *reactive counterviolence* by dominated and exploited people and social groups, generating chain reactions of destructive feelings, attitudes, relations, and interactions; and
- *repressive societal violence* reacting to manifestations of counterviolence and aiming to control it.

At any moment of these processes, and regardless of the phases of the circles, *violence means acts of commission or omission, as well as societal conditions that inhibit the development of individuals, social groups, classes, and entire peoples, by obstructing fulfillment of basic human needs, and unfolding of constructive human energy and potential* (Gil 1996; Fromm 1973).

When analyzing the origins and dynamics of injustice and oppression, we concluded that initiating societal violence was used in establishing unjust and oppressive social orders, and that maintaining and reproducing these orders depends on subtly coercive processes of socialization, as well as on overt and covert, coercive social control. Coercion and societal violence are, therefore, constant features of life in unjust and oppressive societies. Poverty, homelessness, exploitative work, unemployment, inadequate health care, poor education, and individual and social underdevelopment are but some of the symptoms of persistent societal violence of established ways of life in the United States and in other unjust and oppressive societies.

Societal violence is also used by dominant social classes to defend the established way of life against challenges from dominated and exploited classes. Social movements struggling against injustice and oppression are, therefore, likely to encounter coercive and violent measures used against them by the legal system and the armed forces of the established order. It follows that when liberation movements engage in armed struggle, in self-defense against an unjust and oppressive state, or in order to gain control over centers of state power, they are not initiating violence, but are reacting with "counterviolence" to the initiating societal violence used against them by agents of the state (Gil 1996).

Whether coercion and violence are present in liberation struggles is, therefore, a moot question. They are inevitably present as constant societal violence used by dominant social classes to maintain unjust social orders. The proper questions liberation movements ought to consider, when planning their strategies, are, therefore, whether, when, under what conditions, and toward what targets and ends, they should use counterviolence, and whether counterviolence can actually achieve just and nonoppressive social orders.

There can be no universally valid answer to some of these questions since the conditions of injustice and oppression vary greatly in different situations, places, and times, and since strategies of liberation movements need always to be designed in relation to specific societal realities and opportunities. Moreover, only people involved in and affected by particular unjust and oppressive realities, rather than distant supporters and observers, have a moral right to determine what means to use in their struggles. For they alone must live (or die) with the consequences of their strategic choices. To illustrate this important point, outsiders could not have determined the mode of struggle of the American colonists against the British, the revolutionaries against the French monarchy, the ANC in South Africa against the apartheid system, the Bolsheviks in Russia, the Maoists in China, and Castro's movement in Cuba.

Students of social change can, and should, however, examine the consequences of the use of counterviolence in armed struggles in various historic situations. They should also compare the consequences of armed struggles with those of active nonviolent struggles, and they should study theoretical and philosophical positions concerning armed and nonviolent struggles.

Such studies suggest that while armed struggle can be effective in dealing with intense injustice and oppression in the short term, it is unlikely to eliminate domination and exploitation, the root causes of injustice and oppression. It has, at times, overpowered dominant classes that oppress people and benefit from coercively maintained injustice, but it has, so far, not eliminated the practice of domination and exploitation, and is unlikely to do so in the future. It has merely changed the agents and victims of oppression.

The implication of such studies is that armed liberation struggles, whatever their apparent achievements, may have to be followed by long-term, nonarmed, active nonviolent liberation struggles aimed at overcoming the root causes of injustice and oppression rather than merely its most severe manifestations (Bruyn and Rayman 1979; King 1992; Lakey 1987; Sharp 1973, 1979).

Analyses throughout this chapter suggest the following interrelated elements of nonviolent, long-term struggles and strategies to overcome injustice and oppression:

- differentiating short-term goals and emergency measures pursued by social activists in order to reduce the intensity of injustice and oppression, and the suffering of its victims, from long-range goals of comprehensive social transformation, to eliminate the structures and dynamics of injustice and oppression in the fabric of society;

- articulating long-range visions of the essential attributes of just and nonoppressive societies;
- building social movements of activists committed to human equality, liberty, individuality, community, democracy, and harmony with nature, from local to global levels;
- spreading critical consciousness concerning social, economic, political, and cultural realities, human needs and interests, and values and ideologies, through social and professional encounters in everyday life, and in connection with conventional, issue-specific social activism and electoral politics;
- replacing competitive interest group politics with politics of common human needs;
- transforming one's own consciousness concerning people and nature, leading to changes in one's actions, social relations, and life style;
- creating and spreading alternative social, economic, political, and cultural institutions inside established social orders, leading to the gradual replacement of existing unjust and oppressive institutions;
- dealing nonviolently with defenders of the status quo, in societies in which civil and political rights are constitutionally guaranteed;
- engaging in nonviolent, extended, consciousness-expanding social transformation efforts, following armed struggles to overthrow extremely unjust and oppressive governments, to transcend tendencies toward domination, exploitation, and inequalities.

4

Dilemmas and Vicissitudes of Social Work

So far, this book has explored the meaning, sources, and dynamics of injustice and oppression, as well as strategies to overcome these conditions inhibiting human development. Based on these explorations, this chapter traces the emergence and development of social services and social work in relation to injustice and oppression, and to social work's ethical commitment to social justice. Examining these issues involves unraveling the societal context from which the social services emerged, and tracing their dilemmas and vicissitudes over several centuries. As we shall see, social work and its precursors, religious and secular charities and social services in Europe, the United States and countries elsewhere have, indeed, a history replete with contradictory tendencies.

The Social Context of the Emergence of Social Services

Social workers view their mandate as promoting human welfare, i.e., social conditions under which people can *fare well*. They need, therefore, to understand, and strive to overcome, the social-structural causes of human *ill-fare*, i.e., conditions that prevent people from faring well. These causes can usually be traced to the institutional systems societies use to organize necessary work and to distribute goods and services, and social, civil, and political rights. The level of welfare and ill-fare of individuals, social groups, and social classes tends to be a function of the work they do, by choice or by coercion, and of the rights and benefits associated with their particular work.

In accordance with our analysis of injustice and oppression, human ill-fare, of varying degrees of severity, is an inevitable result of coercive initiation and perpetuation of socially structured inequalities, and of domination and exploitation of some people and social classes by others. These coercively established conditions were, in the past, reflected in slavery and serfdom, and are now reflected in "free," though exploitative, wage labor. Socially structured inequalities underlie also the tendency that preferred work, desirable working conditions, and privileged shares of goods, services, and rights were, and continue to be, the prerogatives of dominant classes, while less-preferred work, undesirable working conditions, and inadequate shares of goods, services, and rights, were and are the lot of dominated classes. These societal patterns seem to be the systemic sources of widespread ill-fare, which is reflected in such phenomena as unemployment and poverty; physical, mental, and social pathology; individual and social underdevelopment; and massive waste of human potential. Social services and social work emerged and evolved as societal responses to these manifestations of social ill-fare. Indeed, social welfare services would never have emerged unless social ill-fare had first been initiated and institutionalized by societies (Gil 1992, 1996).

Socially structured inequalities, and domination and exploitation in the organization of work and in the distribution of goods, services, and rights, are also major sources of disincentives to work. People are by nature self-motivated to work when they can do so at their own initiative in cooperation and community with others, when they have rights and opportunities to use materials and knowledge necessary for their work, and when they are free to enjoy the fruits of their work (Applebaum 1992; Pope John Paul II 1982). However, people's natural motivation to work is undermined when they are separated coercively and, subsequently, "legally," from concrete and nonconcrete resources to work with, and when they are consequently prevented to work at their own initiative and discretion, and in their own interest, and are coerced, instead, to work for the benefit, in the interest, and at the discretion, of others. Under such conditions, socially structured work incentives become necessary, including threats and the reality of poverty and starvation, to coerce people to compete for, and carry out, work, which they would never choose freely, do not direct, do not enjoy, and do not benefit from adequately. Reversal of these social-structural disincentives to work is likely to result in the restoration of people's inherent work incentives, and would obviate the need for artificial, dehumanizing work incentives (e.g., work requirements of AFDC, the Aid to Families with Dependent Children program).

Charity and social services evolved in response to people's awareness of, and concerns about, human ill-fare around them, the social roots and dynamics of which they usually did not comprehend. The functions of charities and social services have typically not been to eliminate inequalities, domination, and exploitation, the root causes of ill-fare and of disincentives to work, but merely to reduce and *fine-tune* their intensity, so that people could survive somehow, and established ways of life could be conserved.

Sources of Charity and Social Services

The sources of individual and organized charity, and of private and public social services, include a sense of community and solidarity, carried over from ancient, classless stages of social evolution, as well as social and political imperatives to perpetuate ways of life involving domination and exploitation, structural inequalities, and privilege and deprivation (Kropotkin 1956; Piven and Cloward 1971, 1994; Tawney 1964). Accordingly, the following contradictory tendencies may be discerned throughout the history of charities, social services, and social work:

- a collective memory of human solidarity and of mutual aid, as practiced customarily in early human communities, and, to some extent, throughout history;
- a vague sense of community, identity, and sympathy; and of guilt and fear, when becoming aware of other people's ill-fare and suffering;
- ethical traditions, upheld by organized religions, derived from prophetic messages concerning social justice, brotherhood, sister-

hood, and community, in the Bible, the Gospels, the Koran, as well
as in other non-Western, ancient sacred sources;

- efforts by powerful social classes to conserve the social and political
  status quo, its systemic inequalities, its exploitative organization of
  work, and its unbalanced distribution of material and nonmaterial
  goods, services, and rights;
- pragmatic necessity to assure the survival and reproduction of dominated and exploited working classes, and of unemployed, marginal-
  ized labor reserves;
- efforts by dominant classes to assure discipline at work, in spite of its
  frequently dehumanizing aspects, maintain social stability, and prevent social unrest and revolt by victims of injustice and oppression.

Unjust and oppressive societies had always to devise institutional,
legal, and ideological systems to control their exploited working
classes. Organized religions, charities, social services, and social work
have usually cooperated with dominant classes and governments in
regulating the lives of working and unemployed poor people. They did
so by facilitating survival and ameliorating suffering, often in a stigmatizing manner, while counseling and enforcing submission to social,
economic, political, and cultural realities and expectations.

Dimensions of Social Work Practice

In the context of the above-sketched contradictory sources and tendencies of charities, social services, and social work, their willing or
reluctant cooperation with dominant classes and governments, and the
mandates and functions shaped by this cooperation, have been constant sources of dilemmas for practice, theory, and ideology. Social
workers have, consequently, always vacillated among the following
conceptually distinct, yet overlapping and complementary, dimensions
of practice:

- *amelioration*: alleviating suffering resulting from systemic ill-fare,
  injustice, and oppression, especially among people considered
  "deserving poor;"
- *control*: controlling poor people, regulating their labor, and enforcing changes in their behavior, when they are considered immoral,
  "undeserving," and responsible for their own poverty, due to supposedly personal inadequacies;

- *adaptation*: counseling and "treatment," to facilitate submission and "constructive adjustment" to the "normal" realities of unjust and oppressive societies;
- *reform*: advocating, initiating, and implementing "top-down," incremental reforms of policies and services, to reduce the severity of injustice and oppression, but not to eliminate their root causes in the fabric of societies; and finally,
- *structural transformation*: spreading critical consciousness concerning societal realities, and facilitating involvement of social workers and people they serve, in social movements to overcome the root causes of injustice and oppression.

(Axinn and Levin 1982; Bombyk 1995; Brieland 1995; Ehrenreich 1985; Fisher 1980; Gil 1976, 1992; Katz 1986, 1989; Lubove 1968; Mencher 1967; Piven and Cloward 1971, 1994; Popple 1995; Reid 1995; Reynolds 1964; Ryan 1971; Smith 1995; Trattner 1984; Wenocur and Reisch 1989; Wilensky and Lebeaux 1958.)

The above set of related practice dimensions serves as a framework for the following discussion of selected aspects and phases of the history of charities, social services, and social work.

Amelioration: The spontaneous human impulse to alleviate the suffering of others, be they relatives, neighbors, acquaintances, or even strangers, is the oldest and most durable dimension of individual and collective support for people in need. This impulse was an important factor in the development of voluntary charities organized by religious congregations and associations of citizens, and later on, in the establishment of legally mandated, public social services.

For many centuries, neediness and suffering were considered godgiven, normal conditions of low-status people in societies, stratified rigidly by birth. The essential material needs of poor people tended to be met marginally in such societies, and their suffering was ameliorated somewhat in this way. However, the real causes of their poverty tended to be misunderstood, and no consistent efforts were made to comprehend and prevent neediness and suffering in the future.

Amelioration continues to be an important dimension of contemporary social services for poor people. Soup kitchens for hungry people, shelters for homeless people, and medical care for poor people are among the present expressions of this enduring dimension.

Control: Public control of poor, propertyless, able-bodied people, and conditional, limited public assistance to them, were initiated by statutes in England and in other similarly developed European societies, during the transition to capitalism, in order to deal with the threats of poverty, vagrancy, and begging to social stability. The statutes were designed to sustain the emerging capitalist organization of work, and the dominance of hereditary, as well as new, propertied classes, by regulating relations between workers and their employers, and by providing marginal public assistance to poor people, while controlling their work-related behavior. The close connection between public assistance and public regulation of work, workers, and conditions and relations of employment, is reflected in a series of statutes and "reforms" in England over five hundred years, beginning with the Statutes of Laborers (1349), and continuing with the Statutes of Artificers (1565), the Elizabethan Poor Law (1601), the Law of Settlement (1662) and the Poor Law Reforms (1834).

English legislation in the fourteenth and fifteenth centuries aimed to suppress idleness, vagrancy, and begging. It involved work requirements for poor people and prohibited voluntary assistance to them, as such assistance was viewed as causing idleness and poverty. It also regulated apprenticeships in crafts for poor children.

The Elizabethan Poor Law of 1601 recognized, for the first time, a "positive" state obligation to people in need. It required local parishes to raise taxes to administer public assistance, involving direct grants, in their homes, to unemployable, "deserving poor" people; public, compulsory work programs for able-bodied, "undeserving poor" people; and apprenticeships or foster care for neglected children. These features of the 1601 Poor Law continued to be the basis for public assistance in England for about three hundred years.

The Law of Settlement of 1662 reinforced local responsibility for people in need. It authorized compulsory return of poor people to their former parish of residence, and established residency requirements for assistance, to remove incentives for geographic mobility related to public assistance.

During the seventeenth century, many communities established "workhouses" to put able-bodied poor people to work, but when unemployment became widespread, scanty relief to people in their homes was used instead of placement in workhouses. Also, in the seventeenth century, local parishes used "poorhouses" to care for old, sick, and insane poor people who could not care for themselves in their homes.

The 1834 Poor Law Amendments "reformed" the original Elizabethan Poor Law by intensifying repressive features. The amendments established uniform national assistance standards and prohibited home relief for able-bodied people, leaving the poorhouse as their only source of assistance. It was assumed that people would do anything rather than enter a poorhouse. Another innovation of the 1834 reform was the principle of "less eligibility." This meant that assistance to poor people would always be at a level below the lowest wages. An underlying assumption of the 1834 reforms was that "pauperism" was due to laziness of poor people rather than to a lack of employment opportunities. The law was designed to force people to accept any work, however alienating and poorly paid, in order to avoid the repressive and stigmatizing context of public assistance (Reid 1996).

The development of public assistance in England as measures to "control" working and nonworking poor people reflect social, economic, political, and cultural tendencies associated with the gradual transition of feudalism into early capitalism (Hunt and Sherman 1986; Marx 1977; Mencher 1967; Polanyi 1944; Thompson 1963).

The relatively static conditions of medieval feudalism underwent major changes between the fourteenth and seventeenth centuries. Enclosure of common lands by feudal lords, expulsion of serfs from land they had lived on and cultivated for many generations, and their subsequent, often futile, search for employment and survival, caused increases in the numbers of poor people and vagrants beyond the capacity of individuals, congregations, and communities to ameliorate. Traditional patterns of assistance to people in need were, therefore, gradually replaced by legally mandated, locally administered, public social services.

The poverty and suffering of landless, homeless, vagrant people was qualitatively different from the "normal" poverty of serfs, tied to feudal estates, and working for their lords, as well as for their own survival. The "new" poverty was caused by the coercive separation of people from the traditional sources of their livelihood, as a result of which they were no longer able to eke out a meager existence by cultivating land they lived on by right. Instead, they came to depend on securing employment from entrepreneurs in towns and villages, in return for scanty wages.

The social, political, and economic developments leading to, and resulting from, the transition to capitalism are reflected in the emergence of two antagonistic, but interdependent, social classes:

- a dominant, propertied, entrepreneurial class of merchants and craftsmen, who resided mainly in towns which had become centers of trade and manufacture; and
- a dominated and exploited propertyless class of laborers, who had to depend for their livelihood on employment on the estates of hereditary aristocrats, and in the workshops and businesses of the new propertied, entrepreneurial class.

Relations between the classes of evolving capitalist societies were not based on status of birth as under feudalism, but on supposedly "free and voluntary" employment contracts, which were actually involuntary and often coercive, because of the poverty, dependency, and powerlessness of the workers. The new organization of work, production, and commerce reflected these contractual relations of employment, and several related social structural features, including:

- hierarchic control and supervision of workers and working conditions;
- surplus of workers relative to available employment, forcing workers to compete for scarce employment opportunities;
- unemployment, varying in scope and duration, as a nearly constant feature of the organization of work;
- a wage system, resulting in substandard living conditions for workers at the base, and in the lower levels, of the wage pyramid;
- poverty, varying in intensity, among unemployed workers, as well as among many employed, low-wage workers; and
- widespread systemic ill-fare and individual and social pathology and underdevelopment.

The poverty and social ill-fare of growing numbers of landless, homeless, unemployed workers, and vagrant beggars came to be widely perceived as a social problem threatening "law and order," and requiring public intervention, based on legislation, rather than spontaneous, voluntary, charitable acts by individuals, religious congregations, and citizens' associations. Traditional amelioration was, therefore, withheld, by law, from "able-bodied" poor people of working age, who were defined as "undeserving poor," and was available only to people who were defined as "deserving poor," such as widows and their young children, old and sick people, and people with disabilities, i.e., people who were not expected to support themselves through their own labor (Katz 1989).

Since the early stages of capitalism in England, a key feature of public assistance has been to defend and conserve the societal status quo, by dealing with symptoms of systemic ill-fare rather than with its causes in the fabric of society. This approach reflects misconceptions concerning causes and effects. Poverty and dependency were assumed to result from attributes of poor people rather than from social, economic, political, and cultural dynamics; and helping poor people was assumed to perpetuate their poverty. Lack of employment opportunities was typically overlooked, and when it was acknowledged occasionally, no effective measures were taken to deal with it. Instead, able-bodied people who did not find work, were punished, stigmatized, and forced into workhouses, as if unemployment was their fault.

The principle of using public assistance to control the involvement of "undeserving poor" people in society's work system was brought to the American colonies by the early settlers. It has continued to influence the administration of financial assistance and social services on local, state, and federal levels in the United States to the end of the twentieth century. To understand the evolution and current dynamics of public assistance and social services in this country, it is, therefore, necessary to take into account the enduring influence of the *control* dimension of the English Poor Laws, and of the mentality underlying them.

Adaptation: The "control" dimension of social services originated, quite fittingly, in the culture of early capitalism, in the traditional, class-conscious, hierarchic English society, on a settled and populous island. The "adaptation" dimension, on the other hand, evolved, equally fittingly, in a society of immigrants, on a vast, thinly settled, underpopulated continent, richly endowed by nature. This society had evolved an ideology of equality, classlessness, antiauthoritarianism, democracy, and liberty, in spite of massive contradictions, such as destruction of native peoples and cultures, slavery, capitalism, and plutocracy. Moreover, the United States, which was established following a revolt against England's colonial rule, experienced a century of unprecedented opportunity for geographic, social, and economic mobility. There was a subtle message implicit in this history, and in the realities of westward expansion, free enterprise, industrialization, urbanization, and immigration, as well as unemployment, poverty, and human ill-fare: "adapt, fit in, join the mainstream, Americanize in the melting pot, and you, too, can share in the American dream."

Adaptation is actually a sophisticated, more humane version of control. The control and adaptation dimensions of social services are, therefore, to be understood as a continuum rather than as discrete tendencies. Links and interactions among these dimensions can be traced in policies and programs designed for poor people, and implemented by public authorities and voluntary charities in the United States, since the founding of the nation.

The control dimension tended to be dominant in local, state, and federal financial assistance programs, especially following the passage, in 1935, of the Social Security Act, which defined old and disabled people, and dependent children as entitled to support. Controls became particularly intense and punitive through work requirements for "undeserving poor people," such as unmarried mothers and able-bodied individuals of working age (Katz 1986, 1989; Reid 1996; Trattner 1989).

The adaptation dimension, on the other hand, was more pronounced in the programs of voluntary charities, such as "out-door relief" in poor people's homes; "in-door" relief and supervised work in almshouses; counseling by volunteer "friendly visitors," and later on, by professional social workers; and social, educational, and cultural services to neighborhood residents by "settlement houses."

The founding of the United States did not eliminate many problems of the colonial period, including poverty, which came soon to be viewed as a source of crime and social unrest, requiring public measures beyond amelioration and control. Investigations by various state legislatures concluded that the Poor Laws, and especially out-door relief, carried over from the colonial era, were actually causing poverty by tempting people into permanent dependency. These conclusions led to recommendations to establish "perfect institutions" for poor people where stable work and orderly environments would transform them into useful and productive citizens (Rothman 1971).

The above recommendations acknowledged, by implication, that poverty was related to social conditions, as well as to personal short-comings. They also reflected an optimistic view, that people could be reformed in the "right environments." The belief in people's capacity to change through social interventions, fit well into the mentality of the young nation, according to which technical solutions could be designed for almost any problem.

During the early decades of the nineteenth century, many alms-houses were built to care for poor people and to facilitate their adaptation to social realities and expectations. However, the institutions did not achieve the expected results, because of inadequate public support, (a reflection of typically negative attitudes toward poor people), and because immigration and economic crises caused the numbers of poor people to increase far beyond the capacity of almshouses to absorb them.

By the middle of the nineteenth century, poor people were once again assisted mainly in their homes, by local communities, and by a growing number of voluntary charities. Poverty was again viewed as due primarily to personal causes rather than to social conditions, and poor people were being helped, provided they adapted to social realities and conformed to social expectations. Aid was provided cautiously though, and was monitored routinely by "friendly visitors," in order to prevent permanent dependency, and to encourage socially "correct behaviors."

The emphasis of voluntary charities during the nineteenth century on adaptation of poor people to social realities and expectations, through monitoring and moral guidance by friendly visitors, led gradually to a new philanthropic philosophy, "scientific charity" (Lowell 1884). Aiming to balance and integrate amelioration, control, and adaptation, scientific charity involved the following principles (Alexander 1996):

- detailed investigation of applicants for relief;
- a central system of registration, to prevent duplication of services to the same applicant from different charities;
- cooperation among various charities to coordinate their services; and
- extensive use of volunteers as "friendly visitors."

As scientific charity spread across the country, it stimulated the development of professional social work and of university-based professional schools of social work. These developments resulted in the replacement of volunteer friendly visitors by "social case-workers," paid staff members of social agencies, educated in the arts, sciences, and skills of helping people adapt to realities beyond their control (Lubove 1968). These paradigmatic changes of social services in the United States were initiated and nurtured along by local Charity Organization Societies, the originators of scientific charity, and by their national association, the National Conference of Charities and Corrections, which was established in 1879 and transformed into the National Conference of Social Work in 1917.

As social work evolved and matured as a profession during the twentieth century, adaptation became increasingly its dominant dimension. However, control continued to be a subtle aspect of practice, especially in public settings, where it tended to be overt rather than subtle.

There were several reasons for the emphasis on adaptation. One was that the philanthropic agencies in which social work was practiced, and the schools of social work, where it was taught and where its theories were developed, were controlled by social and economic classes, who did not question the established social order, and who defined and shaped the functions of the agencies and schools accordingly. Another reason was that social workers and their organizations were eager to achieve professional status, prestige, and privilege. Advocacy of social change to eliminate injustice and oppression, and practice involving commitment to social justice, were not compatible with these aspirations. For such advocacy and practice would have been in conflict with the interests of wealthy classes who sponsored the agencies, where social workers were employed, and the schools, where they were educated. Moreover, in their consciousness, social workers, like most people socialized in the culture of the United States, tend to view established ways of life as essentially valid (apart from specific correctable shortcomings), and as relatively permanent. Therefore, helping poor and troubled people to adapt to these ways, and to function more effectively within the established social order, seemed to most social workers a reasonable direction for the profession to take.

Finally, during the nineteenth and twentieth centuries, advocacy of social change was often perceived by governments and by the public in the United States as a threat to "law and order" and as "un-American." People involved in movements for social change were, at times, subjected to repression, and many social workers who shared radical perspectives tended to keep their political views separate from their practice. Moreover, schools of social work, social agencies, and professional associations of social workers conceptualized practice as politically neutral.

For the reasons noted above, social work practice and theory came to be influenced increasingly by psychology, psychiatry, and by medical models of disease and cure, and to a lesser extent by sociology, economics, and theories of social change. As to practice, growing numbers of social workers came to identify as "therapists" who help people to adapt to existing conditions rather than as "agents of social change" who would help people to organize, in order to adapt existing conditions to human needs. During the second half of the twentieth century, the identification of social workers with therapy and with psycho-therapists came to be reflected in a shift from working with poor and low-income people in voluntary and public social agencies, to working with middle and high-income people, in "private practice," using the medical profession as a model.

The above sketch of the evolution of social work and its dependence on powerful social elites, reveals the sources of the contradiction between the social justice commitment of the *Code of Ethics*, and the dominant tendency of social work practice, to facilitate adaptation to the realities of injustice and oppression.

Reform: While adaptation helps people to live with existing realities and to conform to "normal" societal expectations, reform pursues reductions of injustice, oppression, and ill-fare, but avoids confronting their institutional sources. Social reforms are usually initiated by enlightened members of dominant, privileged classes as concessions in response to social unrest, caused by long-standing injustice and oppression. The social class dynamics of reform efforts in the United States are illustrated by the New Deal response to social unrest and fear of revolution during the Great Depression of the 1930s, and by marginal antipoverty measures in response to riots in many cities during the 1960s and 1990s.

Efforts to reform unjust and oppressive conditions began probably soon after the emergence of societies based on domination and exploitation in human relations. The sacred scriptures and teachings of ancient religions, and the mythology and legislation of many early communities and empires contain ample evidence of top-down reform efforts (Durant 1935).

In the United States, social reform efforts go back to the beginnings of the nation. They include well-intentioned, yet unsuccessful experiments, in the nineteenth century, to establish "perfect institutions," to care for and rehabilitate poor people and convicted offenders, and to treat mentally ill individuals (Rothman 1971). They also include relatively effective efforts, by the federal government, following the Civil War, to help freed slaves and veterans of that war (Bentley 1970; Skocpol 1992). And they include social policy reforms initiated by Charity Organization Societies in accordance with "scientific charity" principles (Katz 1986; Lowell 1884).

Pursuit of social reforms by members of dominant classes, in reaction to the appalling conditions of poverty in urban slums, was the essence of the "Progressive Era" in the United States during the late nineteenth and early twentieth centuries (Crunden 1982; Hofstadter 1955). Social services were involved in the reform efforts of the progressive movement mainly through the settlements and their National Federation, organized in 1911 (Carson 1990; Davis 1984; Lundblad 1995; Reid 1996; Smith 1996).

Settlements began to spread across the country since about 1885, about the same time as Charity Organization Societies. These social service movements differed profoundly in philosophy and practice. Yet, in spite of their differences and conflicts, they became, eventually, the main sources of professional social work, and also of the enduring ethical dilemmas of the profession.

Since their founding, settlements were deeply committed to social reforms and engaged consistently in advocacy, while also providing services in their neighborhoods, to ameliorate poverty and ill-fare, and to help people adapt to prevailing realities, pending the eventual implementation of reforms. They also initiated systematic research into the social conditions of their communities, to develop knowledge necessary for effective advocacy.

Charity Organization Societies, on the other hand, expected social workers on their staffs to help people adapt to social realities, and to exercise subtle controls toward that end, but not to engage in reform activities in their roles as agency employees. When charity societies pursued social reforms, responsibility for advocacy was assumed by board members and executives. Research by charity societies tended to study the history, "diagnosis," treatment, and outcome of individual cases, but not overall social and economic conditions associated with the difficulties of the individuals and families they served.

Settlement residents and leaders understood that poverty and ill-fare were caused mainly by social injustice and oppression, intrinsic to the dynamics of capitalism in the United States, rather than by personal attributes of poor people. They realized that people's attributes were largely the effects of social and economic dynamics, and of the culture and values, which shaped these dynamics. They assumed that people could change, and would become productive citizens, when their social and economic conditions were transformed, and when they were assured stable opportunities for working and living with dignity. In accordance with these assumptions, residents of settlements related to people around them democratically, compassionately, and respectfully, as neighbors and citizens rather than as inferior beings to be reshaped and controlled.

The idea of settlements was originated by Samuel Barnett, a parish priest who founded Toynbee Hall in London's East End slum. It was brought to the United States by educated and committed individuals, who had visited Toynbee Hall, including Stanton Coit, founder of the Neighborhood Guild in New York, Jane Addams, founder of Hull House in Chicago, Robert Wood, founder of Andover House in Boston, Lillian Wald, founder of Henry Street Settlement in New York, and Ada McKinley, who founded Southside Settlement House in Chicago and began a tradition of African American women in Settlement House leadership. According to Smith (1996):

> Settlements were places where students, ministers, and humanitarians "settled" (hence the name) to interact with poor slum dwellers with the purpose of alleviating the conditions of capitalism. Those conditions included a poor working class formed by the migration of people from the country to crowded cities; from agricultural Eastern Europe to an

industrializing America; and from a rural, defeated South to a rapidly commercializing, urbanizing North. Depending on the character of its neighborhood, the charisma of its leader, and the source of its funding, settlement work ranged from direct aid for children and indigents to organizing people for social justice.

Many people from dominant classes, who wanted to participate in struggles against social injustice and oppression, for political, ethical, and religious reasons, joined settlements as residents and community workers. Julia Lathrop and Grace Abbott, first and second Chiefs, respectively, of the U.S. Children's Bureau, are but two among many future leaders of social work and social reform, who lived and worked in settlements during early stages of their careers, and gained thus deep insights into the realities and dynamics of poverty, injustice, and oppression (Lundblad 1995).

Settlements and their local and national leaders participated in social reform efforts of the progressive movement concerning public health, public housing, urban parks, women's suffrage, consumer protection, labor and child labor legislation, etc. While focusing on discrete issues, in accordance with conventional politics, they developed nevertheless, a holistic perspective on social ills. They were well aware of links among different manifestations of injustice, and of their common sources in established social, economic, and political institutions. They understood that the well-being of children, families, and communities depended on stable work and adequate income, and that social reforms would eventually have to be pursued in an integrated, rather than a fragmented, manner. They believed in active, rather than laissez-faire, government, and they knew that profit-driven "free enterprise" without constraints and regulations would not automatically assure the well-being of all people.

These insights led the progressive movement and leaders of settlements to advocate for, and to achieve, regulation of selected domains of social life. On the federal level, regulations were formulated and implemented concerning interstate commerce, antitrust legislation, civil service and merit system requirements, banking, and monitoring of foods and drugs. On state and local levels, reforms through regulation dealt with children's and women's work, wages, housing, fire codes, zoning laws, public health, food processing, merit employment requirements, and reforms of politics, including provisions for referenda and recall (Reid 1996).

Another reform concept, Jane Addams and other leaders of the progressive era pursued, was to replace means-tested, stigmatizing charity with a system of social insurance. This meant collectivizing normal risks of life, such as loss of income due to illness, accidents, death, retirement, and unemployment, through regular contributions to a publicly administered fund, which would provide benefits to people experiencing insured risks, without investigating their resources and "worthiness." This approach to social reform originated in Europe, late in the nineteenth century, and was implemented in the United States, first through workers' compensation legislation, enacted by most states during the second decade of the twentieth century, and later on through the Social Security Act, which became federal law in 1935, as part of the New Deal response to the Great Depression.

Ever since the Great Depression and the New Deal, social reform has become a major focus of social work and social services, equal in importance to amelioration, adaptation, and social control. The depression had devastating consequences for individuals and families from all social classes, and many people came to realize that economic forces affected everyone, and that no one was immune to the risk of loosing one's livelihood under capitalism. Poverty was no longer seen as the lot of only marginal groups of the population, due largely to supposedly personal defects, but as the potential fate of nearly everyone. Government interventions in the economy, in accordance with the theories of Lord Keynes, a leading English economist, came, therefore, to be widely accepted as necessary, in order to promote a stable economy, and to prevent social unrest.

Following World War II, the profession of social work moved beyond the "main-stream" consensus, which favored limited government action to sustain a healthy economy, toward a progressive, social reform position, which expected government to develop positive policies and programs, conducive to the optimal development of individuals, families, communities, and social groups. However, the social reform orientation of many social workers and their professional organizations did not lead to a resolution of their ethical dilemmas and contradictions. For, while they consistently advocated reforms conducive to healthy human development, they usually neither acknowledged, nor challenged, the roots of individual and social underdevelopment, i.e., the structures of injustice and oppression in contemporary capitalist societies and cultures.

Moreover, in spite of the reform rhetoric, which echoed the philosophy of the New Deal, the actual practice of most social workers, in public and voluntary social agencies and in private practice, continued to be shaped largely by amelioration, adaptation, and control dimensions. This resulted, inevitably, in contradictions between the realities of practice, on the one hand, and the social justice mandates of the Code of Ethics of Social Work, and the social policy advocacy by leaders of the profession, on the other.

Structural Transformation: This evolving, controversial, and marginal dimension of social work practice and theory overlaps with the reform dimension, but also transcends it. Its aim is to pursue transformation of the systemic roots of injustice and oppression rather than merely reduction of their intensity. Structural transformation aims also to overcome the ethical dilemmas and contradictions of social work by helping people not only to alleviate their unmet needs, but also to develop critical consciousness concerning social realities, and to organize and act against destructive societal conditions that obstruct fulfillment of their needs. In this sense, the structural transformation dimension of social work corresponds to the primary prevention dimension of public health, for it is concerned with the identification and eradication of the causes of social ill-fare rather than merely with the neutralization of symptoms.

Structural transformation tendencies can be discerned in prophetic challenges to injustice in the scriptures of ancient religions, including Jewish and Christian sources, important aspects of the culture of the United States. Pursuit of social justice through structural transformation, one of the Bible's contradictory themes, is illustrated in obligations to free slaves, to cancel debts, and to redistribute accumulated wealth during jubilee years. It is also reflected in the concept that land may not be owned individually, as it belongs to God, and through God to all the people (Leviticus 25).

In the Gospels, Jesus is quoted urging a wealthy man to distribute his wealth to poor people, and, when the man hesitates, Jesus observes that it was easier for a camel to go through the eye of a needle than for a wealthy man to enter into the kingdom of God (Matthew 19). Following Jesus's crucifixion, his disciples lived communally, having "all things in common," and sharing their possessions and goods, "as every man had need," prefiguring Marx's notion, "to each according to need" (Acts 3; Tucker 1978).

Transformation of unjust and oppressive social institutions into just and nonoppressive alternatives has been advocated throughout history, not only by prophetic, religious movements, such as liberation theology in the twentieth century, but also by secular, humanistic, and socialist philosophers, who examined the meaning of human existence and the conditions of ethical human relations (Barry 1973; Boff 1986; Buber 1958; Dewey 1935; Freire 1970; Fromm 1955; Rawls 1971; Rousseau 1967; Tawney 1964; Tucker 1978). Influenced by religious social justice advocacy and by humanistic and socialist political thought, social workers have repeatedly developed approaches to practice oriented toward the elimination of injustice and oppression, mainly during periods of economic crises and social unrest (Bailey and Brake 1976; Bombyk 1995; Corrigan and Leonard 1978; Fisher 1980; Galper 1980; Gil 1976, 1979; Mullaly and Keating 1991; Piven and Cloward 1994; Rein 1970; Reynolds 1964; van Kleeck 1991; Wagner 1990; Wineman 1984; Withorn 1984).

Pioneers of the social justice tendency among social workers were the residents of settlement houses around the turn of the century. Their social change efforts included community and trade union organizing, occupational safety and health legislation, labor legislation, health insurance, women's suffrage, and peace. Through coalitions with progressive movements, they achieved important social reforms, despite strong political opposition.

Pursuit of social change attracted many social workers during the depression of the 1930s. They organized Rank and File, a socialist movement critical of New Deal programs, which preserved the capitalist institutions and culture of the United States. They also organized unions among social service workers, published a radical journal, *Social Work Today* (1934–1942), initiated local political discussion clubs, and supported labor unions and organizations of unemployed workers. Among the activists of the Rank and File movement was

Bertha C. Reynolds, a social work teacher and author who, in 1938, was asked to resign as associate director of the Smith College School of Social Work, because of her socialist and union activism. Ms. Reynolds became later the first social worker of a labor union, the National Maritime Union.

World War II and political repression during the "cold war," and especially during the McCarthy era, led to a marked decline of progressive activism among social workers, many of whom suffered from persecution and were forced to keep their political views to themselves (Andrews and Reisch 1996).

During the 1960s, a social justice orientation reemerged among social workers, under the influence of the civil rights, peace, and feminist movements. Social workers became involved in community organizing in antipoverty and Model Cities programs, and in the Welfare Rights movement. These unconventional practice experiences led to a renewal of a radical critique of capitalist society and culture, and of the control and adaptation dimensions of conventional social work. The critique stimulated the founding of local networks of radical human service workers and of a socialist journal, *Catalyst*, which was published by a social workers' collective for about ten years, before being reorganized in 1988, as *The Journal of Progressive Human Services*.

In 1985, a national society of progressive social workers was founded, the Bertha Capen Reynolds Society. The goals of this society include development of theories and practice of social-change-oriented social work, and support for radical human service workers, who are often isolated in social service settings that emphasize social control and adaptation rather than social transformation.

During the final decades of the twentieth century, tendencies to preserve the status quo of injustice and oppression intensified in the politics, economy, and culture of the United States. Similar tendencies were also spreading in Europe and on other continents, and economic insecurity, social unrest, and armed conflict affected many societies. In the United States, social policies and social services, on local, state, and federal levels became major targets of conservative political forces and were, and continue to be, severely affected by them.

However, in spite of these developments, progressive social workers continued to pursue the ethical goals of social justice and freedom from oppression, through practice and collective study, and through movement building and political activism on local levels and beyond. The emerging theoretical premises of their practice, and illustrations from that practice in different settings and contexts, are discussed in chapter 6.

To avoid misunderstandings, it is important to note, in ending this chapter, that the foregoing discussion of the dilemmas and vicissitudes of social work has not addressed the "microlevel" of direct social services, but only the "macrolevel" impact of the profession on systemic injustice and oppression. The quality of practice was not examined, but only the overall social function and aggregate effects. Hence, the critique refers only to the overall function and aggregate effects of social work, but not to the quality of direct practice.

The entire discussion examined whether social work practice has been consistent with the mandate of its *Code of Ethics*, to pursue social justice and resist oppression. The answer seems to be that although social workers and their organizations tend to abhor injustice and oppression, they usually do not challenge their systemic sources in capitalist dynamics. Moreover, in actual practice, in spite of their values and ethics, social workers are typically not involved in efforts to confront and transcend injustice and oppression, and their roots in the fabric of society. They tend to consider their practice as politically neutral, and they separate it, therefore, from their philosophical rejection of injustice and oppression.

PART TWO

Implications for Policy, Practice, and Organizing

5

Transition Policies Beyond Poverty, Unemployment, and Discrimination

This chapter addresses short-term and intermediate-range transition policies to end poverty and reduce the intensity of injustice and oppression prior to eliminating their sources in the fabric of society. Transition policies differ markedly from long-term strategies aimed at eliminating the systemic causes of ill-fare and at transforming unjust institutions into just alternatives. However, they also overlap with, and complement, long-term strategies, for they are necessary steps toward a comprehensive transformation of the institutions and culture of unjust and oppressive societies.

Transition policies are necessary since comprehensive transformations involve lengthy processes in time rather than brief revolutionary moments. Social movements, pursuing such transformations, require, therefore, interim goals to initiate and sustain the process of transcending prevailing destructive social realities.

Moreover, transition policies to reduce deprivation and suffering are not only necessary as interim goals, but are also ethically valid in their own terms. Movements for social justice must never disregard, and must always aim to alleviate as fast and as much as possible, human suffering due to existing injustice and oppression. Activists should, therefore, pursue simultaneously the long-term goals of comprehensive liberation along with meaningful transition policies, the implementation of which seems feasible in the context of prevailing cultural and legal conditions. Contradictions between transition policies and structural transformation can be dealt with, when social movements are clear about the differences, overlaps, and complementarities between short-range, intermediate, and long-range goals, and avoid advocating ameliorative measures as substitutes for long-range goals.

Transition policies should be designed to reduce deprivation caused by prevailing social injustice, to enable people to live under less alienating conditions while they struggle for fundamental transformations. They should also be designed as "nonreformist reforms," to test and expand the "normal limits" of the prevailing social order, so as to serve as stepping stones toward the long-term goals of comprehensive human liberation (Gorz 1964).

Useful sources for transition policies are the Economic Bill of Rights, proposed by President Franklin Roosevelt in his State of the Union message to Congress on January 11, 1944, and the Universal Declaration of Human Rights, adopted by the United Nations, without dissent, on December 10, 1948, with the active support of the United States (Harvey 1989; Wronka 1992; UNCHR 1992; see appendixes A and B for the text of these documents).

Roosevelt's Economic Bill of Rights was intended to complement the civil and political rights, guaranteed by the Bill of Rights of the U.S. Constitution, with economic rights, without which civil and political rights cannot usually be fully exercised. His proposals included rights to useful paid employment, adequate income, and decent housing; adequate medical care and the opportunity to achieve and enjoy good health; adequate protection from the economic fears of old age, sickness, accident, and unemployment; a good education; fair terms of trade for the products of farmers; and freedom from unfair competition and domination by monopolies at home and abroad.

Roosevelt's proposals were not enacted into law by the U.S. Congress. However, the United Nations Universal Declaration of Human Rights, which is gradually being perceived as customary international law, includes nearly all the economic rights Roosevelt advocated. It is, in fact, the first international human rights document that does not assume that civil and political rights can be assured and exercised in the absence of economic rights. It, therefore, asserts civil and political rights, not apart from, but in the context of, comprehensive economic rights.

Movements pursuing social justice could introduce into the political arena, as transition policies toward their long-range goals, proposals to eliminate poverty by expanding economic rights in accordance with the Universal Declaration of Human Rights and Roosevelt's far-sighted proposals. Advocacy of such transition policies could steer political discourse away from conventional interest group competition toward politics of common human needs and human rights, the real interests of every human being and every social group (Maslow 1970; Towle 1945). Such a reformulation of political objectives and discourse could initiate durable, political alliances among oppressed groups and people committed to social justice, in place of temporary, tactical coalitions of conventional politics.

Rights, Opportunities, and Responsibilities to Work

Most important among transition policies to end poverty and to transcend the vicious circle of meaningless reforms of stigmatizing public welfare are the elimination of involuntary unemployment and the assurance of rights to adequate income (Gil 1986). Rights and opportunities to useful and meaningful work would have to be assured, by constitutional amendment or statute, to everyone able and ready to work. Furthermore, all people would have to be guaranteed by law an adequate income, at least at the level of the actual cost of a decent standard of living, earned by their work, or received, as an entitlement, through government transfers, when unable to earn a living for reasons such as age, sickness, disabilities, caretaking responsibilities, etc. Implicit in these legally guaranteed rights would be corresponding responsibilities to work and to share in the production of goods and services, to meet the needs of the entire population.

Rights, opportunities, and responsibilities to work, and rights to adequate income are universal human interests, regardless of gender, age, race, and other human attributes. The proposed legal rights and responsibilities are, therefore, not intended to thwart the real human interests of any person, group, or class in society, whatever their current circumstances, but are meant to facilitate everyone's development, to enhance the quality of life for all, and to promote a sense of security, dignity, social harmony, and cooperation (Applebaum 1992; Collins et al. 1994; Gil and Gil 1987; Pope John Paul II 1982). Rights and responsibilities to work are certainly compatible with the "work ethic," an important aspect of the culture and ideology of the United States, which is actually not sustained by the prevailing work system and by established public policy, in spite of consistent rhetorical support (Rodgers 1979). People can hardly be expected to live by, and conform to, a work ethic, as long as involuntary unemployment is not eliminated.

People are usually not aware that rights to work and to adequate income are actually implicit in the U.S. Constitution. Article VI of the Constitution defines treaties, ratified by the United States, as "Supreme Law of the Land." One treaty ratified by the United States in 1945 is the United Nations Charter, which obligates member nations "to promote: (A) Higher standards of living, full employment, and conditions of economic and social progress and development . . . and (C) Universal respect for, and observance of, human rights and fundamental freedoms for all without distinction as to race, sex, language, or religion" (Articles 55). Furthermore, the Universal Declaration of Human Rights, referred to above (appendix B), lists work and adequate income among the fundamental human rights, to be upheld by all signatories (Article 23). It follows that actions by the Federal Reserve Bank to avoid inflation by maintaining a supposedly "natural" rate of unemployment (of about five percent) seem to be in conflict with the Constitution and with international obligations of the United States (Gil 1995).

"Full employment," i.e., participation in the production of socially necessary goods and services by everyone ready to do so, seems clearly a feasible transition policy, which could be implemented within the capitalist economy of the United States, by the following measures:

- Periodic adjustment by Congress of the legal length of individual work time (day, week, year): The purpose of such adjustments, which Congress has the authority to make, would be to maintain an approximate match between the number of work positions in the economy and the number of available workers. Thus, for instance, the aggregate product of about 100 million workers, working eight hours per day, would require the work of over 114 million workers, were the standard work day reduced by one hour, a gain of about 14 million positions (Gil 1983; Schor 1992).

- Publicly sponsored production of socially necessary goods and services: When private firms do not produce certain necessary goods and services because of insufficient profit, governments, from local to national levels, could sponsor their production. This would create additional work positions, while meeting real needs of people for housing, health care, education, environmental protection, maintenance of infrastructure, etc.

The feasibility of implementing "full employment" by shortening individual work time and redistributing work, and by creating additional work through public sponsorship of socially necessary production, indicates that obstacles to ending unemployment are neither economic nor technical, as is widely assumed, but are essentially political. These obstacles seem due to the fact that employers tend to benefit materially from an oversupply of readily available labor, and that they are, therefore, interested in maintaining involuntary unemployment, regardless of destructive consequences for individuals, households, communities, and the entire economy. The material benefits for employers result from decreases of wages and corresponding increases in profits—a typical result of competition for work among unemployed workers.

One further consequence of competition among unemployed workers who differ in gender, race, age, and other characteristics, which should be mentioned here, is discriminatory attitudes and practices such as sexism, racism, ageism, etc. These destructive attitudes and practices are unlikely to be overcome at their roots, as long as unemployment is accepted as a "natural" economic phenomenon.

The transition policies sketched above concerning rights, opportunities, and responsibilities to work, and rights to an adequate income are derived from the following related insights:

- work is an essential aspect of life, for without it, life can neither be sustained nor its quality enhanced;
- the main sources of the "real" wealth of societies are the capacity of its people to work, along with material and knowledge resources created by work, rather than "capital" and money;

- work to sustain and enhance life is an inherent human need, fulfillment of which, in a meaningful and self-directed manner, seems
  essential for individual development, self-respect, social recognition,
  and a sense of security, identity, and belonging to a community;
- people are unlikely to realize their potential, when their societies
  exclude them from constructive participation in socially necessary,
  useful production; and
- social development from local to global levels tends to be obstructed,
  and aggregate human wealth is reduced, whenever individuals and
  groups are excluded from participation in work.

The foregoing insights suggest that human work may have to be
defined as mental, physical, and emotional processes, necessary for,
and conducive to, the maintenance of life and the enhancement of its
quality. This definition could eventually replace the one implicit in the
concept of the Gross National Product (GNP), according to which
only remunerated employment in the production of goods and services is counted as work. In accordance with the suggested redefinition, activities which reduce the quality of life, may have to be redefined as "counterwork," and be phased out from being counted in the
GNP.

The suggested redefinition of human work has important, though
controversial, implications for work systems and for the implementation of transition policies concerning rights and responsibilities to
work, and rights to adequate income. Activities such as caring for children by parents, and caring for people with disabilities by their relatives, seem certainly socially necessary work and may have to be
included, therefore, in the work systems of societies. Men and women
undertaking such work, by choice or by necessity, rather than seeking
employment outside their homes, may eventually have to be remunerated adequately out of public revenues, secured through appropriate
modifications of the tax code (Gil 1992, Technical Appendix). On the
other hand, activities judged to be counterwork, e.g., production of
nuclear weapons, to use an extreme example, may eventually have to
be phased out.

These notions may seem utopian in the prevailing political, economic, and ideological context of the United States. However, they are
gradually being incorporated into social policies of some countries in
Europe and elsewhere. Furthermore, acting on recommendations of

the 1985 World Conference of Women in Nairobi, the UN General Assembly resolved, later that year, to urge member nations to include the unremunerated work of women in their GNP accounts. Legislation to comply with this resolution has been passed by the European Parliament in 1993, and has also been introduced in the United States Congress in 1991 and 1992 by Representative Collins of Michigan with endorsements by the Congressional Women's Caucus and the Congressional Black Caucus (Gil 1992, Legal Appendix; *Los Angeles Times*, March 25, 1993).

The inclusion in the work system of our society of publicly sponsored production, care-taking functions by parents and relatives, and, possibly, other life-enhancing activities, such as academic and vocational studies, artistic and literary pursuits, as well as the exclusion of life-inhibiting counterwork, would cause important modifications of the substance and the aggregate scope of socially necessary work. These changes would have to be taken into account when designing and implementing the proposed transition policies concerning universal rights and responsibilities to work and rights to adequate income.

Adequate Rather Than Minimum Income

Elimination of poverty requires not only transition policies concerning rights, opportunities, and responsibilities to participate in socially necessary work, including caretaking work. It requires also policies defining the meaning of "adequacy," and assuring adequacy of wages for work, and of entitlement income for students, for people temporarily unemployed, while searching for work, and for people whose capacities to work are limited due to age, disabilities, and ill-health.

To be adequate, wages, as well as transfer income out of public revenues, would have to correspond, at least, to the actual costs of a decent standard of living as measured through periodic consumer and market surveys. The Bureau of Labor Statistics used to conduct such surveys routinely, but early in the 1980s they were suspended as a cost-saving measure. These surveys would have to be reinstituted as a basis for defining and maintaining the adequacy of wages and transfer income (U.S. Dept. of Labor 1967). Transition policies linking levels of wages and entitlements to a legally specified adequate standard of living would prevent erosion of purchasing power and decline into poverty as a result of inflation.

Child Care as a Shared Responsibility of Parents and Society

To assure to women and men equal rights and opportunities for meaningful work and career development, the care of children may have to be conceptualized as a shared responsibility of parents and society. Shared responsibility would require not only a system of caretaker wages for parents, as suggested above, but also public financing of high-quality child care services for preschool children, and after-school centers for school-age children. Parents who choose to use publicly financed child care for their children, on a part-time or full-time basis, in order to pursue education, paid work, and careers, would have to forgo all, or part, of publicly provided caretaker wages.

Once publicly financed child care services and a system of caretaker wages would be established, all parents would be able to arrange the care of their children and the pursuit of work and careers in the same way affluent parents are free to do now.

Allowances for Children, Students, Unemployed and Retired Workers, and People with Disabilities

As a further transition policy to eliminate poverty, a universal children's allowance, paid out of public revenues to children under a specified age (e.g., from birth to high school graduation) could be established, as has been done in many countries for many decades. The amount of this allowance could correspond to the real cost of supporting a child, and could be linked to changes in the cost of living. The children's allowance would replace dependency deductions for children under the prevailing tax code, an indirect children's allowance, which results in unfair advantages for children in households with higher income. The proposed children's allowance is intended to assure the adequacy of income for large households, as the prevailing wage system does not take into account differences in the size of households (Burns 1968).

Just as children could be protected against poverty by means of a universal children's allowance, similar income guarantees to prevent poverty could be established for students in post-secondary academic and vocational schools, for retirees, for sick people and for people with disabilities, as well as for people unemployed temporarily, while looking for work. These public income guarantees could eventually replace Social Security (which is financed through a regressive payroll tax), public welfare programs, loan and grant scholarship programs, as well as food, energy, and housing assistance programs.

The purpose of the allowances and income guarantees suggested above is to assure adequacy of income for everyone, but not to increase the income of higher income groups. Therefore, the allowances and income programs would have to be considered "taxable income" in order to recoup parts or all of the amounts from households with higher overall income.

Health Services

Elimination of poverty through the transition policies sketched above is expected to improve significantly the physical, mental, and social health of people and communities. However, preventive and curative health services, providing universal coverage, would nevertheless be necessary, also after the elimination of poverty. A "single-payer" health care system, financed through general revenues, but administered in a democratic, decentralized, cost-conscious fashion, may, therefore, have to be established. This system would have to stress prevention and early diagnosis of physical and mental illness, and high-quality patient care throughout the country's urban and rural areas. Such a universal health system could eventually replace and transform Medicare, Medicaid, Government Health Care for veterans and elected officials, as well as the entire array of "for profit" and "not-for-profit" health insurance and health care organizations.

Tax Reform

Implementation of the antipoverty transition policies suggested above would require appropriate reforms of the tax code. Guiding principles for these reforms would have to be that every household be entitled to a tax-exempt income up to the level of the actual cost of an adequate standard of living. Income above that level, regardless of its source, would have to be taxed, at progressively increasing rates, to support adequate levels of public services and investments.

Eliminating "legitimate" tax shelters, and privileged tax treatment for corporations and for capital gains, as well as phasing out public welfare programs and the regressive social security system and its separate payroll taxes, could result in a simple and fair tax code, and in adequate tax yields, to support the proposed antipoverty transition policies along with other necessary government services.

Tax reforms, incorporating the principles sketched here, would make it possible to "balance" government budgets, by matching revenue levels and tax rates to democratically established levels of public spending for socially necessary governmental functions. This would enable the government to avoid deficit spending, borrowing, and interest payments (which tend to benefit mainly wealthy investors in government bonds), without causing "human deficits," by reducing and eliminating services and investments conducive to, and necessary for, healthy human development.

Beyond Short-Term Transition Policies: Quality and Choice of Work

Once rights, opportunities, and responsibilities to work, as well as rights to adequate income will have been assured to all, intermediate-range transition policies could be pursued concerning the quality of work, and people's rights to freely choose their occupations. These issues are important in terms of the quality of people's lives, but they are unlikely to be dealt with effectively in the political arena before rights to work and income are assured to all.

Work would have to be redesigned to be meaningful, rather than alienating, and conducive to the physical, mental, and emotional development of workers. Systems of production involving hierarchical controls, divisions between design, management, and implementation functions, and fragmentation of work into minute, monotonous, and meaningless steps could be transformed into integrated models, comprehended, designed, controlled, and managed by suitably educated and trained workers themselves. Implicit in such a transformation of work would also be a gradual shift from individual and corporate ownership to worker and community control of productive enterprises and resources.

To overcome conventional practices of channeling dominated and discriminated against social groups and classes into less desirable, development-inhibiting work, all people would have to be assured equal rights to choose their work, and to change to different lines of work throughout life. Such shifts among occupations could be facilitated through lifelong access to education during "sabbaticals," vacations, or evening and weekend studies. Redesign and humanization of production processes could transform many now undesirable occupations into desirable ones, and might broaden the range of occupations that people would choose freely.

Ideally, all socially necessary work would be made sufficiently attractive to be chosen voluntarily by enough people. However, work deemed socially necessary that could not be redesigned and humanized, and that would, therefore, not be chosen voluntarily by enough people, would have to be shared by all people on a rotation basis. This could be done through a community service system which everyone would have to join for a specified time, perhaps upon graduation from high school. Desirable work, chosen by too many people, may also have to be rotated among all those interested in it, and educated for it.

Transition Policies and Changes in Values and Consciousness

Enactment and implementation of the antipoverty transition policies sketched in this chapter would require consistent efforts by social movements to facilitate shifts in the dominant values of the culture of the United States and in the consciousness of its people. Values would have to shift on the following policy-relevant dimensions listed in table 5.1.

Dominant social values, individual consciousness, and the societal institutions they sustain do not change easily. They are unlikely to change in response to moral arguments. Values and consciousness tend to be rooted in perceived needs and interests of people and tend to change, therefore, when people's perceptions of their needs and interests undergo reexamination and revision.

TABLE 5.1 Policy-Relevent Value Dimensions

Current Positions	Future Positions
inequality	equality
domination and exploitation	freedom from domination and exploitation
individualism and disregard for life and dignity of others	individuality and affirmation of life and dignity of others
disregard of community	affirmation of community
competition, from individual to global levels	cooperation, from individual to global levels
disregard for the environment	harmony with the environment

To bring about value changes in the United States from currently dominant toward suggested future positions, large numbers of people would have to discover that their economic, social, psychological, spiritual, and security needs cannot be met adequately within the established societal order, and that transition policies conducive to everyone's human development could, therefore, serve their real interests. Spreading such insights seems to depend on consistent efforts by social movements to support the emergence of critical consciousness concerning people's real needs and interests, through nonviolent, dialogical processes.

6

Social-Change Oriented "Radical" Practice

Can social workers, while helping people deal with diverse social problems, act also as agents of fundamental social change, aimed at overcoming injustice and oppression? There are no easy answers to this question, but growing numbers of social workers and educators, in the United States and elsewhere, think that a social change, or "radical" orientation, could be integrated into everyday practice (Bailey and Brake 1976; Galper 1980; Gil 1976, 1978, 1987; Reynolds 1985). Doing so could eventually resolve contradictions between the conventional tendency of social work, to help people adjust to the status quo of domination and exploitation, and the ethical imperative, to confront injustice and oppression.

To transcend conventional social work practice and function as agents of social change, social workers require theoretical and philosophical perspectives, and practice principles, different from those now dominant in the profession. They also require an attitude of experimentation and critical consciousness toward their practice, and they need to help one another to evaluate it, and to deal constructively with resistance from administrators, supervisors, and colleagues in organizations practicing along conventional lines. Support-and-study groups of radical social workers who often feel isolated in their places of work, and networks of such groups, can facilitate mutual help among practitioners.

The first two sections of this chapter discuss and illustrate theoretical and philosophical perspectives and practice principles of radical social work. Support-and-study groups are the subject of the third.

Theoretical and Philosophical Perspectives and Practice Principles

Radical social work is based on the following assumptions concerning human nature, human needs, individual and social development, social evolution, people's relations to their natural environment, and physical, emotional, and social health and ills.

Assumptions Underlying Radical Practice

Human nature and human behavior: Human nature does not compel specific behaviors of people, except for certain instincts and reflexes. Rather, nature sets limits within which people may choose and change their behaviors. A broad range of attitudes, behaviors, and social relations is possible within these limits along a continuum between constructive and destructive poles. People's actual choices of particular behaviors, along this continuum and within the biologically given limits, tend to be influenced by the dominant values and institutional dynamics of their societies and cultures, and by changes, over time, in these values and institutional dynamics (Gil 1992).

Human needs, development, and health: Common human needs include biological-material, social, psychological, creative-productive, security, self-actualization, and spiritual dimensions. When people can realize their common needs in their natural and socially shaped environments, their development tends to proceed spontaneously. Physical, emotional, and social health result from stable fulfillment of human needs, while social problems and human ills reflect failure to meet these needs (Fromm 1955; Gil 1992; Maslow 1970).

Human needs and social order: Social orders may be understood as specific designs for meeting human needs, which people evolved and transformed, by interacting with one another and with their natural environments, in pursuit of survival. At any stage of history, social orders involve relatively stable, yet gradually changing, patterns of policies and values concerning the following *operating variables* of human societies:

a. stewardship of natural and human-created resources;
b. organization of work and production;
c. exchange and distribution of goods and services, and of rights and responsibilities;
d. governance; and
e. biological, social, and cultural reproduction.

The policies and values that shape these variables regulate through their combined effects the following *outcome variables*:

a. the circumstances of living of people and social groups;
b. the relative power of people and groups;
c. the mutual relations of people and groups; and
d. the overall quality of life in societies.

By regulating the conditions and quality of life of people, their relative power and their human relations, the policies and values of a society influence the extent to which people can realize their common needs, the scope of their development, the state of their physical, emotional, and social health, as well as the scope of overall social development (Gil 1992).

Social-structural violence and nonviolence: Societies whose policies and values tend to obstruct, i.e., "violate," people's development, by consistently frustrating fulfillment of their common human needs, may be considered "structurally violent." On the other hand, societies whose policies and values tend to be conducive to needs fulfillment, and hence, to human development, may be considered "structurally nonviolent" (Gil 1996).

Roots of social problems: It follows from the foregoing assumptions, that social problems, which people experience, as individuals and as members of particular social groups, and which they bring to social workers, are usually rooted in prevailing societal institutions, policies, and values rather than in inherent attributes and shortcomings of people. While these problems can often be ameliorated through social work interventions with individuals, groups, and communities, their solution and prevention seem to require modifications of institutions, policies, and values, in ways conducive to the fulfillment of common human needs (Fromm 1955; Gil 1992; Ryan 1971).

Social problems and individual responsibility: It is important to note here that radical social workers do not disregard the possible contributions and responsibilities of people concerning the problems they experience. However, since people do not exist in a social vacuum, and since their personal attributes evolve through continuous interaction with societal dynamics, solutions of existing problems and the prevention of future ones require, in the view of radical practitioners, not only personal efforts toward responsible functioning, but also restructuring of social and economic institutions. Social work practice ought, therefore, to pursue constructive functioning of people within prevailing destructive realities, as well as appropriate changes in dysfunctional social institutions (Bailey and Brake 1976; Reynolds 1985).

People's capacities to adapt societies to human needs: As suggested above, people originated and are always reproducing the institutions, policies, and values of their societies, through cooperative and competitive interactions. They seem, therefore, to have the capacities to transform these institutions, policies, and values through collective efforts, in order to assure their compatibility with common human needs and with the requirements of healthy human development (Freire 1970; Gorz 1967).

Principles of Radical Practice

From the foregoing assumptions and theoretical and philosophical perspectives, radical social workers have derived the following set of practice principles:

Rejecting political neutrality and affirming politics of social justice and human liberation: Radical practice ought to contribute openly and consciously to political struggles for social justice and human liberation. This principle differs from the conventional view that mixing politics and practice is unethical and unprofessional, and that practice ought, therefore, to be politically neutral. In accordance with the norm of political neutrality, many social workers view politics as a domain apart from practice, and tend to consider participation in politics a private affair, to be engaged in only away from their practice settings.

Analysis suggests, however, that political neutrality is an illusion since social work practice usually has political roots and consequences, regardless of the intentions and consciousness of practitioners. Political neutrality would require that practitioners neither support nor challenge the societal status quo. Yet, not challenging an existing social order means actually supporting it tacitly rather than being neutral toward it. Hence, neutrality in itself is a political act, for it transforms practice into a subtle tool for supporting the status quo, while preventing it from becoming a tool for challenging it. Political support for the status quo rather than neutrality is also implicit in the view of many social workers, that people's problems are mainly due to individual shortcomings, as well as in practice approaches based on this view, which support adaptation to prevailing social realities.

Since political consequences of social work practice seem thus unavoidable, though practitioners may not be aware of them, the view that mixing politics and practice is unethical and unprofessional, seems invalid. It would, therefore, be more appropriate, in ethical terms, to replace unintended, covert political aspects of practice with consciously chosen overt ones, and to hold social workers accountable for their political choices and for the consequences of these choices. An appropriate political choice for radical social workers would be a commitment to social justice and human liberation.

Affirming values: Just as radical practice cannot be politically neutral, it also cannot be value-free, for social work practice either reflects and upholds the dominant values of society, or rejects and replaces them. Radical social workers would, therefore, have to reject the notion of value-free practice. They would have to choose consciously values that are opposed to those which shape existing, unjust, and oppressive institutions.

The core values of radical social work would, therefore, have to be equality, liberty, cooperation, and affirmation of community in pursuit of individual and social development. People would have to be considered equal in worth and dignity, in spite of individual and cultural differences, and they would have to have equal rights and responsibilities in all spheres of life, and be free from domination and exploitation (Tawney 1931). These values seem crucial for radical practice, since the problems people bring to social workers tend to result, directly or indirectly, from societal dynamics shaped by values of inequality, selfishness, competition, domination, and exploitation.

Transcending technical/professional approaches: Radical social workers need to transcend technical/professional approaches, fragmented by fields of service, and concerned mainly with relieving symptoms and facilitating coping under prevailing social conditions. While these are valid and important short-range objectives, they do not confront the roots of social problems in the fabric of society. Social problems are usually not isolated fragments, to be overcome by "technical and professional fixes," but symptoms of the totality of particular ways of life. Radical social workers need to help people trace the links between their particular problems and the dynamics of their ways of life, and to support them in confronting the problems at their roots.

Facilitating critical consciousness through dialogue: An appropriate medium for radical social work practice, regardless of function, level, and setting, is an emancipatory dialogical process. Such a process involves a sensitive exploration of problems, as experienced and perceived by people; supportive measures designed to ameliorate these problems; and help with unraveling links between the perceived problems and their societal roots and dynamics (Freire 1970).

Emancipatory dialogue is also intended to facilitate insights into human nature, into the shaping of social realities by people, and into people's capacities to change and reshape these realities. It also aims to help people affirm their worth, dignity, rights, and potential collective power, and to support them in the pursuit of fundamental solutions to their problems, through involvement in social movements that struggle against injustice and oppression. Dialogical process must never deteriorate into indoctrination, for its ultimate aim is to facilitate emergence of critical consciousness through sensitive, supportive, liberating, nonauthoritarian, and nonhierarchic relationships.

Advocating human rights: Another important principle of radical practice is advocacy, aimed at assuring the exercise of all rights to which people are entitled under prevailing policies. However, these policies do not grant adequate rights, for they have shaped the very conditions under which people's problems have emerged and continue to be regenerated. Advocacy by radical social workers would, therefore, have to transcend demands for implementing existing rights. It would have to present demands for equal rights, responsibilities, and opportunities, and would have to challenge policy proposals which tend to be mere variations on ancient themes of inequality, domination, and exploitation.

Confronting obstacles to needs fulfillment: Radical social workers consider the fulfillment of common human needs and the development of people's innate capacities the goal of just and free societies. They would have to facilitate, therefore, insights into obstacles to need fulfillment and human development in "violent" social structures, such as coercively established and maintained, exploiting and alienating modes of work and systems of rights distributions. Based on these insights, they would have to advocate transformation and redesign of prevailing systems of work and rights distribution, in ways conducive to unobstructed human development (Gil 1996).

Gaining insight into personal oppression: Radical social workers would need to explore whether, in the prevailing social realities, they too may be unable to actualize their innate potential; whether their individual development may also be inhibited; and whether they too may be victims of dominating and exploiting, social, economic, and political dynamics, though in different forms, and to a lesser extent than the people they serve. They may realize through such explorations that they too have a personal stake in human liberation and social equality, and that they would have to identify with oppressed people, including the ones they serve, and join their struggles and movements, rather than identify with dominant classes and their institutions, values, and policies.

Furthermore, they may conclude that they would have to transcend prevailing formal divisions between themselves and the people they serve, divisions reflective of conventional concepts of professionalism and expertise, according to which education, competence and skills entitle people to privilege, authority and higher social status.

Prefiguring future possibilities: Radical social work would have to involve efforts to transform the style and quality of practice relations and administration in social services from vertical, authoritarian, nonegalitarian patterns toward horizontal, participatory-democratic, egalitarian ones, as far as this is possible in prevailing realities. Every space within existing settings, which radical practitioners can influence, could be transformed to reflect alternative possible human relations. In this way, elements of alternative realities, or prefigurations of future possibilities, could be created experimentally, within existing service organizations, by and for the providers and users of the services.

Unions and support-and-study groups of social workers could incorporate elements of such prefigurations and could link up with local and translocal networks of social movements for human liberation. Undoubtedly, such efforts and experiments are difficult to carry out. They are likely to involve risks, resistance, and conflicts, since they test and try to expand the limits of what is possible within prevailing social realities. Such testing and expansion of limits are, however, essential aspects of liberation processes (Gorz 1967).

Spreading critical consciousness and building social movements: Finally, radical social workers would need to initiate dialogue with colleagues concerning workplace, practice, and social justice issues, in order to spread critical consciousness concerning these matters. They would also have to organize unions and support-and-study groups at their workplaces, and they would have to participate in social and political action and movement building within and beyond their local communities.

Illustrations of Radical Practice

Direct Clinical Practice

The following sketch of protective services for abused and neglected children and their families illustrates the use of the theoretical and philosophical perspectives and the practice principles of radical social work in direct, clinical practice.

Many social workers in child welfare and child protection services view abuse and neglect of children as due mainly to personal attributes of their parents or parent substitutes. They consider these caretakers, therefore, responsible for incidents of abuse and neglect in which they were involved, and expect them to change or lose custody of their children.

My studies of child abuse and neglect led me to conclude that the abuse inflicted upon children by society exceeded in scope and destructive consequences their abuse and neglect by parents (Gil 1970). I also realized that abuse of children by their parents is frequently associated with abuse of the parents by society. Such "societal abuse" tends to affect millions of families through unemployment, discrimination, poverty, malnutrition, homelessness, developmental deficits, ill-health, inadequate education, and social deviance, as well as through stressful conditions in everyday life, especially at places of work.

In spite of these circumstances, protective service workers usually convey, explicitly or implicitly, punitive and threatening messages to parents and caretakers who are involved in incidents of abuse or neglect. The essence of these messages is that parents are "bad," for if they were not, their children would not be abused and neglected. Furthermore, unless they changed and corrected their child-rearing patterns, their children would have to be removed from their homes. Such messages, even when expressed sensitively by skilled social workers, tend to result in antagonistic relations between parents, social workers, and protective services.

Implicit in these messages are claims that society is "good," is concerned about children, and is free from guilt regarding their conditions. Reality is different, however. Society, as now constituted, is guilty of massive child abuse and neglect since prevailing social policies doom millions of families to conditions that make adequate child care nearly impossible (Ravo 1996).

Radical social workers, on the other hand, understand child abuse as "counterviolence" by troubled parents and caretakers, who react to "societal violence" which obstructs the fulfillment of their common human needs. Such "societal violence" is viewed by radical practitioners as intrinsic to unjust and oppressive societies whose institutional systems involve domination and exploitation (Gil 1996).

While child abuse and neglect tend to occur not only in the context of poverty, but also in contexts of economic stability and affluence, these latter incidents, too, can usually be traced to social and cultural dynamics which inhibit the realization of the nonmaterial needs of perpetrators. Human needs are, after all, multidimensional. They include, as already noted, not only material-biological needs, but also social, psychological, productive-creative, security, self-actualization, and spiritual ones (Maslow 1970).

Radical social workers do not condone abusive and neglectful acts. They reject such acts unequivocally and will say so to parents without hesitation. However, they avoid threatening and punitive messages, for they do not reject the parents who are trapped in vicious circles of societal violence and counterviolence, as victims and as perpetrators. Moreover, radical social workers are aware that many parents who are involved in incidents of abuse and neglect do love their children, want them to grow up into "successful" adults, and are themselves deeply hurt by the aftermath of maltreatment in their families.

Radical social workers are concerned, not only with the safety and well-being of abused and neglected children, but also with that of their families. Their long-range goal is to prevent future abuse and neglect by eliminating their societal and personal sources and dynamics. Their short-range goals are to work with parents to assure the well-being of their children and families, to help them gain insights into the sources and dynamics of abuse and neglect, and to involve them in efforts of social movements aimed at overcoming societal violence, the root cause of maltreatment of people of all ages.

Generalizing about radical social work practice in child protection is difficult, as each case is unique. However, certain general themes may be noted. Radical social workers begin their work with parents involved in abuse and neglect, by encouraging them to talk about their children, their living and working conditions, and about links, they see, between these conditions and the abusive incidents. They acknowledge the parents' love and hopes for their children, and the stressful realities of the conditions they describe, which interfere with their love and hopes. They admit readily that they themselves might not be able to provide better care for children, were they to live in the parents' conditions, and they explore with the parents concrete avenues toward reducing stresses in their lives, and assuring the safety of their children. They also share with the parents their political perspective, involving rejection of values and policies which shape the prevailing conditions of injustice, oppression, and needs frustration.

Dialogues, exploring these themes sensitively, in a nonthreatening manner, aim to enable parents to move beyond defensiveness and guilt, to affirm their love for their children in spite of ambivalent feelings that led to their abuse and neglect, to redirect their anger toward the sources of their own abuse in social conditions and dynamics, and to mobilize their energies and resources for dealing constructively with their own and their children's short-term and long-term needs. These dialogical encounters are expected to result in trust between parents and social workers, emergence of a critical consciousness concerning social realities, self-empowerment, and gradual involvement in collective efforts of social movements challenging unjust and oppressive conditions.

Working with parents who abuse and neglect their children tends to be difficult in spite of the insights of radical social workers and their accepting attitude toward such parents. For parents who have been hurt deeply by society may hesitate to trust social workers who are agents of the very society that has hurt them and continues to do so. Radical social workers understand and expect these difficulties and they avoid reacting angrily. They know that patience and consistent support over extended periods of time are necessary, so that parents may risk eventually to move toward a relationship of trust.

The theoretical perspectives and practice principles of radical social workers conflict, inevitably, with the laws and policies that regulate protective services for abused and neglected children, and with social work practice approaches which are derived from these laws and policies. Radical practitioners need to face these conflicts openly and honestly, with the agencies that employ them and with the parents and children whom they serve, rather than pretend to conform to agency policies and act covertly against them.

One should not expect an easy resolution of conflicts between theoretical perspectives and practice principles shaped by opposing values and politics. However, by facing these conflicts openly, and by consistently advocating alternative perspectives and approaches, radical practitioners might initiate dialogues with colleagues, supervisors and administrators. Such dialogues could eventually contribute toward changes of public policies and agency practices. Also by acknowledging these conflicts and discussing alternative values, policies, and practices with the people they serve under existing laws and policies, radical social workers could further the development of trust and critical consciousness.

The themes which radical social workers explore through dialogue with families of abused and neglected children, and the internal logic of these themes, are also relevant to other direct services, such as family and children's services, public assistance, mental health services, school counseling, personnel services, and court and correctional services. These themes are also applicable, with appropriate, common-sense modifications, to practice with groups and communities. The themes can be summarized systematically as follows:

- exploring issues and solutions people present;
- helping people trace links between their issues and individual, social, economic, political, and cultural dynamics;
- acknowledging people's strengths, and helping them to move beyond defensiveness, guilt, and self-blame toward self-affirmation and self-empowerment;
- supporting people's use of their own energies and resources, along with available social services, toward meeting their human needs;
- supporting development of trust between people and their social workers;
- facilitating emergence of critical consciousness concerning personal and social realities, and concerning people's capacities to change these realities through collective action;
- discussing openly the social worker's political views and values in opposition to domination and exploitation, the sources of societal violence, and of individual and social problems;
- helping people channel their frustration and anger, caused by societal violence, into constructive involvement with organizations and movements pursuing social justice and human liberation.

These themes do not constitute a standard blueprint for radical clinical practice, but merely a set of general guidelines, to be adapted flexibly, with common sense, to different settings and situations. Blueprints, it needs to be noted, are actually undesirable, for they tend to inhibit creativity, experimentation, and self-direction by practitioners. Radical practice can be developed effectively only through individual and collective creativity of practitioners in different services, who are committed to a radical political perspective and to corresponding social ends. Social workers who have developed critical consciousness, have gained political and economic insights and philosophical clarity, are committed to social justice and human liberation, and consider the people they serve their equals in needs, rights, and responsibilities, seem well prepared to adapt and test radical approaches to different service settings and to the circumstances of people using the services.

Education for Radical Social Work

Schools of social work prepare their students usually for practice in accordance with the status quo–maintaining tendencies of many social service agencies. However, growing numbers of teachers in these schools aim to educate students to confront injustice and oppression through practice, as demanded by the Social Work Code of Ethics. The tentativeness of the theoretical perspectives and principles of radical social work has inhibited its integration into the programs of schools of social work. However, from my own experience and that of colleagues, I know such integration is possible in many schools, though it is neither simple, nor free of costs and risks.

Teaching radical practice involves intellectual as well as experiential dimensions. While substance and teaching style are often considered separately, they are but two related dimensions of a unified process, especially in the study of injustice and oppression. Experiences of students should, therefore, support their intellectual efforts, as in these studies style becomes substance, and the "medium is indeed the message" (McLuhan 1967).

Universities and professional schools are important components of oppressive and unjust societies. They facilitate the maintenance and ideological justification of elitist social orders, and they credential new members of the elites. Their own rules and practices in relation to students, teachers, and staff contain oppressive and unjust aspects.

When teaching about oppression and injustice in universities, radical teachers need to acknowledge and analyze the oppressive and unjust aspects of their institutions, and need to transform their own classes into "liberated spaces," to the extent that "academic freedom" permits. To accomplish this, teachers need to surrender to students responsibility for their studies by eliminating teacher-set requirements and assignments, and by encouraging students to set these themselves. Similarly, students, with advice from teachers, need to evaluate their learning and also grade their work, as long as grading is required.

The role of teachers in a nonoppressive context needs to be that of facilitator, adviser, resource, and nonauthoritarian, critical assistant, rather than "expert," authority, and judge. Learning needs to occur through collective dialogical explorations rather than through top-down instruction. If teachers will consistently yield control to students for their education, students will have opportunities to experience and explore the meanings and dilemmas of responsibility and freedom, and they will be able to study the conceptual issues of oppression and injustice, not as mere abstractions, but as concrete aspects of social relations in everyday life. Under such conditions, education can actually become a liberating experience.

It needs to be stressed, that the educational approach sketched here does not imply abandoning responsibility, initiative and leadership by teachers. Rather, it implies clarity concerning the responsibilities of students and teachers, and fulfillment of their respective parts of a shared undertaking (Burstow 1991; Freire 1970).

The aims of radical social work education, like those of radical practice, include the development of critical consciousness concerning socially shaped realities, and the discovery of oneself as a potentially creative, productive, and self-directing human being in relation to community, society and nature. Such critical consciousness and self-awareness tend to emerge within cooperative, nonhierarchical settings in which teachers act as colleagues in pursuit of knowledge. In such settings learning can be mutual and dialogical rather than one-directional, and learning goals, requirements, and evaluations can be worked out cooperatively by students and teachers.

Teachers, based on their past and ongoing studies, need to map out and recommend domains for study, facilitate the dialogical learning process, suggest appropriate sources and projects, consult with students on individual learning goals, respond critically and constructively to students' projects, and facilitate student evaluations of their learning. Implicit in the educational philosophy and teaching style suggested here is the assumption that progress toward a free, just, and democratic society of the future, requires creation, in the present, of counterrealities to domination and control, to enable students to experience prefigurations of self-direction in the here and now of the classroom (Freire 1970).

The style of radical social work education sketched here involves dilemmas for teachers. One dilemma concerns reactions of students to the absence of controls and to the expectation that they assume responsibility for self-direction of their studies. For most students this would be a new experience, different from previous schooling as well as from experiences in other classes in which they are concurrently enrolled. Reactions tend to range from frustration, uncertainty, and helplessness, to constructive and enriching learning and personal growth. On balance, over many years, I have been encouraged by student response, especially once I overcame my own fears, doubts, and hesitation, and pursued this approach consistently. One constructive way to deal with this dilemma is to use expected and actual reactions of students to this teaching style as opportunities for exploring the meaning, costs, and benefits of self-direction and freedom.

Another more difficult dilemma concerns tensions and conflicts with colleagues resulting from the introduction of a radically different educational philosophy and style into a school. An appropriate frame of reference for coping with this dilemma is the commitment to "academic freedom" shared by faculty members. Being open about what one believes and does, asserting one's right to teach in accordance with one's educational philosophy and values, and respecting the different philosophies, styles, and values of colleagues, may eventually bring about a measure of mutual tolerance, especially when students respond favorably to one's classes and style. However, I do not mean to suggest that it is easy to cope with this dilemma.

The substantive domains which students need to explore in preparation for radical practice are implicit in the theoretical perspectives and principles of such practice. They include conditions and dynamics of human development and well-being, obstacles to development, and sources and dynamics of human ill-fare. This requires studying human nature, human needs, and human development, social evolution throughout history, and the consequences of variations in social organization for human development and well-being.

Students need also to examine the social, economic, cultural, political, and ideological contexts of life in their countries, and the conditions of different social groups and classes. Studying these issues requires a historical perspective.

Having explored prevailing realities, their roots and evolution, and their consequences for health and ills, students need to address philosophical and value issues with reference to alternative societal futures. This could be followed by explorations of personal values and interests in relation to personal history, experiences, and goals.

The domains sketched here require the study of sources from the social and natural sciences. These sources ought not to be studied as separate disciplines, however, but as complementary perspectives on the processes of human life in nature and society.

Major additional foci of study are, of course, social policy, social services, and social work practice. In these studies, it is important to differentiate between short-range and long-range needs and goals, and between "first-aid," adaptation, and prevention foci. It is also important to transcend symptom-related fragmentation of social ills and social services, and to overcome the widespread tendency to separate studies of clinical practice and of social policy by discerning interactions between these levels of intervention.

Finally, in preparation for radical practice, students ought to explore the philosophy of science and research approaches suitable to the development and testing of radical practice and its underlying theoretical perspectives.

Having already noted some dilemmas related to the style of radical teaching, dilemmas related to its substance need also be considered. One major dilemma is that there is so much to cover that no teacher, choosing this approach, should expect to do it all. The reason there is so much to study, is that preparation for radical practice does require an entire "alternative" curriculum, including studies of theoretical foundations and practice, as well as analysis and critique of conventional scientific foundations, assumptions, and service approaches. There is no solution to this dilemma other than to acknowledge it, to introduce students to the various domains they ought to explore, and to motivate them to continue the process of study and critical experimentation as an integral aspect of responsible practice.

A related dilemma is that most teachers cannot achieve competence in the many substantive domains to which students need to be exposed. Here too, the solution is to acknowledge this reality, and to guide students to appropriate sources. Of course, teachers are also students, and need to aim, over time, to broaden and deepen their own knowledge, experience, and competence.

An analysis and critique of conventional teaching in one's own school pose one further dilemma. One constructive approach in dealing with this could be to note that views on social issues and human action are usually not valid in an absolute sense, but rather in relation to particular assumptions and values. Different teachers and students view the world and human life from different perspectives, and arrive, therefore, at different "truths." A further approach to this dilemma could be to note that differences in time perspective may validate different interventions. Thus when people are hungry they need bread, but may not be ready to explore the causes of hunger, and when they are unemployed they need work, and they may have little patience to explore strategies toward full employment. In this sense a radical orientation is not a negation, but an expansion of conventional approaches, which tend to focus mainly on "first aid" and short-range solutions.

One more dilemma is presented by the isolation and loneliness experienced by teachers, students, and practitioners, who pursue a social-justice and liberation orientation. Philosophically, they inhabit a different universe of discourse than many of their colleagues, and consequently they have to link up with similarly oriented individuals and groups in other schools and workplaces in order to develop mutually supportive and affirming relationships.

Social Policy Analysis, Development, and Advocacy

Conventional policy analysis, development, and advocacy tend to focus on "single" issues, e.g., hunger, homelessness, crime, domestic violence, teenage pregnancy, minimum wages, urban decay, environmental deterioration, etc. The usual declared aim of policies formulated around single issues is to eliminate or ameliorate supposedly separate social problems. While amelioration of discrete problems is certainly possible and desirable, elimination is unlikely, since apparently separate social problems are but different symptoms of underlying common causes. Unless these common causes are addressed, the problems are unlikely to be overcome.

A further shortcoming of conventional policy practice is that major aspects of prevailing institutional and cultural realities tend to be treated as "constants" rather than as "variables." Considering key aspects of the social status quo unchangeable, inevitably limits the potential effectiveness of policies designed to deal with such problems as unemployment and poverty, which are "normal" phenomena of capitalist societies. Social problems associated with the dynamics and culture of capitalist institutions obviously cannot be dealt with effectively unless new policies were to modify these institutions significantly rather than treat them as constants.

Furthermore, conventional policy analysis frequently lacks causal theories concerning problems targeted for intervention. In the absence of insights into the sources and dynamics of social problems, analysts tend to formulate policies focused on symptoms rather than on causes. Thus, for example, policies designed to deal with crime and violence do not unravel and confront their causes. Rather, based on notions of retribution, punishment, deterrence, and rehabilitation, they expand police forces and prisons, and incarcerate or execute convicted perpetrators (Gil 1996).

Finally, conventional policy analysts and advocates often formulate and pursue policies, the implementation of which they consider politically feasible, given prevailing social, economic, and cultural realities, even when they are aware that these policies are unlikely to deal effectively with targeted problems. Apt illustrations of the consequences of the feasibility orientation of conventional policy practice are President Clinton's efforts to reform health care and public welfare. His search for politically feasible compromises with powerful adversaries, and his hesitation to advocate humane health and welfare policies, around which a popular movement might have been mobilized, resulted in abandonment of the pursuit of universal health care, and in repeal of a long-standing entitlement to minimal support for poor families.

Radical policy practice uses a holistic approach to policy analysis, development, and advocacy. In such an approach, social problems are understood as related symptoms, rooted in a society's way of life, and policies designed to deal with the problems are viewed as interacting elements of its system of social policies. Like all other policy outcomes, social problems are assumed to result, not from separate policies, but from the combined effects of all extant policies of a policy system, and the dominant social values which shape that system. Real changes of social realities and effective solutions of social problems, such as the elimination of domination, exploitation, poverty, and injustice, are, therefore, assumed to require transformations of entire policy systems rather than marginal adjustments of specific policies.

Furthermore, radical policy analysts and advocates consider the institutional and cultural contexts of human societies transient results of interactions among people throughout history and, therefore, subject to change by interactions among people living now and in the future. Accordingly, they treat these contexts conceptually as "variables" rather than as "constants."

A useful conceptual foundation for radical policy practice is a general theory of social policy that identifies the essential *operating* and *outcome variables* of social life and of policy formulation, and that seems applicable to human societies anywhere and anytime (Gil 1992). This theory derives from the study of the human condition in nature and from the realization that, as a result of biological evolution, the human species is genetically less programmed than other species. Humans are born without genetically fixed patterns of life, but with capacities to create, transmit, and transform such patterns, through interaction and communication with each other based on reflection and critical consciousness, and through interaction with the natural environment from which they derive their means of existence.

Because of the lack of genetically transmitted ways of life, social organization could not have evolved unless people had created systems of policies that made the continuous reproduction of their ways of life possible. Policy systems evolved by humans may thus be understood as a substitute for, or an equivalent of, the genetic transmission of programs for living of other species. Each discrete social policy is a human-evolved specification for particular aspects of social life, a contributing element to a society's policy system. And all the policies of a society extant at given stages of its history constitute transient systems of policy which shape its way of life through time.

Patterns of life and the policy systems which maintain them evolved out of people's efforts to survive by meeting their basic needs in particular natural environments. The drive to survive and to develop by meeting basic human needs may, therefore, be understood as the source of energy for the evolution of social organization among humans, and of policy systems to sustain their social orders. *The extent to which people are actually able to meet their basic needs seems, therefore, an appropriate criterion for evaluating the policy systems evolved by different societies, anywhere and anytime.*

To assure their viability, human societies must evolve policies concerning the previously identified *operating* and *outcome variables* of social life, i.e., resources, work, rights, governance, and reproduction; and the circumstances and power of people and social classes, the quality of their relations, and the overall quality of life. The ability of people to meet their basic needs depends always on the way these variables are shaped by their societies.

Human life proceeds simultaneously on the level of action and the level of consciousness. These levels reinforce each other through continuous interactions. As children grow up in particular societies and cultures, they interact with people around them and internalize into their consciousness the particular modes of action and thought of their society and of the social groups and classes to which they belong. Along with the specific patterns of actions and thoughts, people internalize also the values and perceptions of interests of their society, which tend to justify and validate the internalized actions and thoughts, and to reinforce conformity to expected modes of behavior.

The values and perceptions of interest, which people internalize along with their society's ways of life, are products of human interactions and communications throughout history, in the same way as the patterns of life and policies. In societies divided into dominant and dominated classes, the values and perceptions of interest, which people internalize and which shape their actions and thoughts, tend mainly to derive from, and to serve, the interests of the dominant classes, often to the detriment of dominated classes.

The following dimensions of radical policy analysis, development, and advocacy are based on the above-sketched theory of social policy:

- Before actually analyzing or formulating specific policies, one needs to study the issues to be addressed by the policies. This involves exploring the nature and scope of the issues, and causal theories concerning them.
- Next one needs to discern the chain of concrete effects expected to result from the implementation of a given policy, including intended

and unintended, and short- and long-range effects. This involves clarifying overt and possibly covert policy objectives and the explicit and possibly implicit value premises underlying them, as well as the hypotheses guiding the strategies and concrete provisions of the policy. It also involves examining the size and relevant characteristics of target populations, and estimating the extent to which the actual effects of a policy match, or are expected to match, its objectives.

- Once the concrete effects of a policy have been identified, their implications for the structure of society and for the entire system of social policies need to be discerned in terms of expected and actual changes in the previously identified *operating* and *outcome variables* of systems of social policy. This aspect of a policy analysis is its "radical" core, for it is meant to discern changes in the relative circumstances and power of people, social groups, and classes, and in the relations among them. It would, therefore, reveal whether a policy could actually be expected to change the extent to which people are able to realize their basic needs, or whether it would merely be a new variation on the ancient theme of inequalities concerning the satisfaction of human needs.

- The next dimension of an analysis explores the social forces which affect the development and implementation of a policy. An understanding of the interactions between a policy and the social forces in its environment seems necessary in order to estimate the policy's consequences.

- A final dimension of radical policy analysis is the formulation of alternative policies aimed at the same, or at different, objectives concerning the issues addressed. Policies generated in this way, can then be compared and evaluated in terms of:

  - policy relevant value dimensions;
  - attainment of specified policy objectives;
  - implications for social structure and the policy system as a whole;
  - the extent to which human needs can be satisfied;
  - costs and benefits; and
  - possible unintended effects.

The framework for the analysis and development of social policies reproduced in appendix C is designed to facilitate such holistic policy analyses and to examine the following questions:

1. Which societal domain does the policy address?
2. How would the policy affect this domain in concrete terms?

3. How would society's institutions and policy system, and the extent to which people can meet their basic needs, be affected by the concrete effects of the policy?
4. What effects may be expected from the interactions of the policy with various forces within and outside the society?
5. What alternative policies could be formulated concerning the same and different objectives, and how would they compare?

In concluding the discussion of radical policy analysis, it needs to be noted that its goal is not merely to gain thorough insights into policies being debated in the public arena at various times, though this is certainly an important function of radical analysis. Rather, the ethical goal of radical policy analysis, like that of radical education, is to contribute to political action in pursuit of social justice and human liberation by facilitating the emergence of critical consciousness and the building of social movements. A holistic approach to policy analysis, as sketched here, seems well suited to this ethical goal for it is designed to guide analysts beyond:

- focusing on single issues;
- disregarding causal theories concerning social problems;
- dealing with symptoms rather than causes;
- accepting the social status quo as a "constant;" and
- pursuing feasible compromises with forces conserving privilege and deprivation.

To fulfill the ethical purpose of radical policy analysis, policy studies might be carried out in cooperation with local and translocal community organizations and movement groups, which confront injustice and oppression. The results of such cooperative studies and the formulation of alternative policies would need to be disseminated widely.

Effective use of insights from policy studies depends largely on their relevance to the real needs and interests of people. Policies derived from President Roosevelt's proposed Economic Bill of Rights, and from the United Nations Universal Declaration of Human Rights (see appendixes A and B), fit this criterion as they address the human needs and real interests of everyone. Cooperative studies of such foci by networks of radical policy analysts and community groups might serve as a catalyst for expanding critical consciousness and organizing movements.

Support-and-Study Groups of Radical Social Workers

When helping people to cope with individual and social problems, radical social workers aim to help them also to develop critical consciousness concerning injustice, domination, and exploitation—the direct or indirect sources of their problems. In addition, radical practitioners aim to encourage people who use their services, to get involved in movements for social justice and human liberation. Finally, radical social workers strive to coordinate their own professional practice and political activism, with the social change strategies of movements confronting injustice and oppression.

The perspectives, practice, and activism of radical social workers derive from their critique that capitalist institutions, and the culture they sustain, tend to obstruct the development of people by interfering with the fulfillment of their basic human needs; and that real solutions and prevention of social problems depend, therefore, on the transformation of these institutions and cultural tendencies into human-development-conducive alternatives. Many social workers and administrators of social services reject this critique and consider the perspectives of radical social workers, and their approach to practice, unprofessional, unrealistic, and utopian. And some members of dominant social classes, including also members of boards of directors of social service agencies, consider the views and critique of radical social workers not only unrealistic, but also "un-American."

As a result of these negative attitudes toward their views and practice, radical social workers tend to feel isolated and to experience conflicts and dilemmas in their places of work. Coping with these feelings, conflicts, and dilemmas on their own, as some radical practitioners are doing, is inconsistent with a philosophy stressing community and cooperation. Radical social workers need, therefore, to create opportunities for mutual support and cooperation to:

- deal constructively with conflicts and dilemmas at their places of work;
- examine and develop their practice and theory;
- enhance their social and political activism;
- protect their civil rights and professional freedom when administrators fail to do so; and

- organize, and work with, social service unions.

Experience suggests that support-and-study groups that meet on a regular basis, and local and translocal networks of such groups, can indeed help radical social workers deal with the personal difficulties and the intellectual and political challenges related to their work. Thus these groups can enrich their members' professional practice and political activism.

Support-and-study groups can serve as settings for nonhierarchical, cooperative, mutually caring relationships for practitioners who feel isolated and alienated because their values, assumptions, political philosophy, practice theory, and practice approaches differ markedly from those of their coworkers and work settings. The groups can also confirm the "realism and sanity" of radical practitioners which are sometimes questioned by colleagues and administrators because of their unconventional, "deviant" views. Support-and-study groups can thus help radical social workers reaffirm the integrity of their perspectives and facilitate self-empowerment.

Support-and-study groups are also meant to serve as settings for cooperative, critical study and evaluation of the professional practice and political activism of their members. Through such study, the groups can further the development of radical social work practice and theory, in accordance with the Code of Ethics of social work, and the values, goals, and strategies of liberation movements.

Finally, support-and-study groups can enable their members to deepen their political insights and to enhance their critical consciousness by exploring issues such as:

- the meaning of democracy and human liberation;
- the attributes of social, economic, political, and cultural institutions conducive to the fulfillment of human needs and to individual and social development;
- advocacy and strategy toward human liberation;
- integration of political activism into everyday life; and
- coordination of radical social work practice with the strategies of liberation movements.

Support-and-study groups aim to develop an egalitarian, democratic, and dialogical style, similar to, and influenced by, the consciousness-raising groups of the women's liberation movement in this country (Morgan 1970), and the "base communities" of liberation theology in Latin America (Boff 1986; Freire 1970).

In accordance with their dual functions, the meetings of support-and-study groups usually consist of an informal social segment and a planned professional one. The very style of the groups, and the sense of solidarity among their members, are negations of the competitive mode of human relations in many places of work and throughout the existing culture. The groups thus attempt to create "liberated spaces" and prefigurations of alternative patterns of human relations of future, democratic-egalitarian societies.

The informal social segments of group meetings involve spontaneous sharing of experiences at work and in the personal lives of members. This helps members to transcend the usual separation between people's personal and professional lives, and to develop a sense of community.

The professional segments focus on presentation and analysis of samples of members' practice and social activism. Members rotate in assuming responsibility for these presentations. Key issues in the analysis are discernment and evaluation of the "radical" aspects of the practice and social actions members present, and of differences, if any, from conventional, status-quo-maintaining practice.

Analyses by support-and-study groups of their members' work differ from supervision in workplaces because of the equality of status and power among group members, and the absence of hierarchical dynamics. People can feel comfortable talking about their work and activism, including strengths and weaknesses, without fear of negative consequences. Because of the opportunity and freedom to affirm not only constructive aspects of one's work, but also to raise questions and doubts concerning possible shortcomings, discussions, and evaluation of practice in support-and-study groups seem to be more conducive to learning, and to developing practice and theory, than supervision in hierarchical contexts.

Support-and-study groups are concerned primarily with workplace issues of their members, and with the development of radical practice. However, the groups are also concerned with organizing local and translocal social change efforts, this being an essential aspect of the ethical responsibilities of social workers. Involvement in social actions can be either cooperatively by entire groups, or by individual members. Social actions undertaken by individuals can be reviewed and supported by their groups in the same way as their professional practice.

One further function of support-and-study groups is the recruitment of new members, initiation of new groups, and organization of networks. Groups can facilitate recruitment and organizing by sharing their experiences at conferences and writing about them in professional publications. Conference presentations and articles can be planned, written, and delivered collectively, rather than by individuals, to reflect the nonhierarchical relationships of the groups, their affirmation of community, and their efforts to transcend conventional cultural tendencies. The formation of new groups can also be assisted by inviting individuals to participate in meetings of established groups, before encouraging them to organize new ones.

I began this chapter by asking whether social workers could act as agents of fundamental social change, aimed at overcoming injustice and oppression, while helping people deal with their current problems. Implicit in that question was a further query, whether social workers could practice consistently in accordance with the social justice value of their Code of Ethics.

To answer these questions, I examined theoretical and philosophical perspectives of radical social work, and illustrations of radical approaches to direct practice, professional education, and policy formulation and advocacy. I also discussed support-and-study groups which radical practitioners can create in order to support one another and to develop their practice and theory.

Based on these explorations, we can conclude that social workers who are committed to the values of their Code of Ethics could certainly integrate a social justice orientation into their everyday practice, regardless of practice settings and roles. However, we also have to conclude that when they are choosing to do so, they are likely to encounter resistance at their places of work, for radical practice challenges the exploitative tendencies and perceived interests of dominant social classes.

The understandable negative response, in capitalist cultures, to the consciousness-expanding emphasis of radical practice, is well illustrated by the following quote from Dom Helder Camara, Archbishop of Recife, Brazil, an advocate of liberation theology:

> I brought food to the hungry,
> and people called me a saint;
> I asked why people were hungry,
> and people called me a communist.

In spite of widespread resistance to the critique and perspective of radical social work from status-quo-maintaining institutions and dominant cultural tendencies, many practitioners have confronted these obstacles throughout this century, and continue to do so in the present. They are demonstrating, through their ethically committed practice and their social activism, the validity and feasibility of integrating a consistent challenge to injustice and oppression into professional social work (Bailey and Brake 1976; Bombyk 1995; Galper 1980; Gil 1976, 1978, 1987, 1992, 1994; Reynolds 1964).

EPILOGUE

This study has focused on an intellectual paradox of social work. It ends by reflecting on some difficult existential dilemmas that confront anyone seeking to end injustice and oppression.

The Intellectual Paradox of Social Work

The paradox that motivated this work is that social workers are mandated by their Code of Ethics to challenge injustice and oppression, but lack adequate theoretical insights concerning these phenomena and concerning strategies to overcome them. It is obviously not possible to challenge injustice and oppression effectively, when one does not understand their sources and dynamics, but it is possible to profess an ethical commitment to do so without understanding their causes. However, challenge in the context of such inadequate knowledge tends to focus on symptoms of injustice and oppression, such as poverty and homelessness, while avoiding to confront their underlying causes: the dynamics of domination and exploitation which permeate capitalist societies and the culture that sustains them. Social work's challenge to injustice and oppression has usually been limited to fighting symptoms without even acknowledging their causes. This is the essence of the intellectual paradox of the profession, as revealed in this work.

In confronting this paradox of social work, this study aimed to clarify the meaning, sources, and dynamics of injustice and oppression and to discern long-range strategies toward their eventual elimination. The resulting insights make it possible to resolve the long-standing intellectual paradox of the profession by shifting its challenge from symptoms to the actual causes of injustice and oppression.

Existential Dilemmas Facing People Committed to Social Justice

Social workers and their organizations might, eventually, use the findings of this study to refocus their challenge from symptoms to causes of injustice and oppression. Such a shift would, however, take much time. The reason is that targeting causes rather than symptoms depends not only on scholarly logic, but on personal commitment by many individuals to dedicate their lifework to the goal of social justice. A commitment of this kind cannot come about quickly as, in order to make it, people need to transcend difficult existential dilemmas which inhere in the insights emerging from this study.

Understanding injustice and oppression and their sources—domination and exploitation—tends to be fraught with multidimensional existential dilemmas and emotional stress, for it implies the need for people to make significant changes in their ways of life, work, and patterns of social relations. It means therefore exchanging the "bliss of ignorance" for the burden of holistic social knowledge along with difficult new choices, conflicts, and fears.

The nature of some existential dilemmas associated with struggles for social justice is sketched below, as clarity concerning them, and their effects on people's choices to challenge injustice, is necessary in order to transcend them.

In unjust and oppressive societies nearly everyone is a victim, as well as an agent and beneficiary of domination and exploitation, depending on one's position and roles in hierarchically organized, competitive institutions. In other words, nearly all people are now part of the problem, regardless of personal philosophy, and would have to change their ways of life to become part of the solution.

Furthermore, relatively privileged conditions of living of some people and social classes result from direct or indirect domination and exploitation of other people and classes who, consequently, live in relative poverty. These outcomes and relations occur not only within societies, but also among societies on a global scale, due to the domination and exploitation of some countries and peoples by others.

There are no quick and easy strategies to eliminate injustice and oppression within and among societies. Unjust and oppressive institutions have evolved and spread globally, over many centuries and millennia, and they are perceived widely as "natural," legitimate, and inevitable. Also, dominant social classes and nations tend to defend established social relations, institutions, and cultures, which they perceive as sound and fair and as compatible with their interests. Transforming these institutions into just and nonoppressive alternatives is, therefore, likely to require lengthy and difficult processes, lasting many decades or centuries. Acknowledging the need for an extended process of social change does not imply tolerance of the status quo of injustice and oppression. It merely means being realistic and avoiding illusions of quick fixes.

Social workers and others who intend to pursue social justice out of ethical convictions and professional obligations need, therefore, to make long-range commitments. Moreover, they need to realize that their goals may not be attainable during their lifetime, as there are no assured outcomes in struggles against oppression.

Participation in movements for social justice does require contributions of time, energy, and material resources. Activists need, therefore, to be ready to shift resources from personal to social movement objectives. Furthermore, participation in social justice movements does involve risks of being isolated and of being perceived and treated as unrealistic, utopian, and even un-American. Activists need, therefore, to learn to deal constructively with the strains of social-change work.

Transformation of consciousness, of human relations, of personal behavior, of lifestyles, and of professional practice are important dimensions of effective social change strategies. Social workers, and others committed to social justice, would, therefore, have to work toward self-transformation concerning these dimensions.

People are likely to hesitate to become involved in social justice movements because they may fear an unknowable, insecure future; changes in their accustomed ways of life, loss of relatively privileged circumstances of living, and negative personal consequences, were they to become known as activists for fundamental social change. Additionally, people may also have doubts concerning the validity of insights gained through this work, which are likely to be reinforced by the normal messages of the prevailing culture.

Transcending Existential Dilemmas

In spite of the existential dilemmas, which cause people to hesitate to challenge the roots of injustice and oppression, many individuals and movements have struggled against them, ever since domination and exploitation have spread within and among human societies. In searching for ways to transcend these dilemmas, it may help to understand the social reality and the motivation of people who succeeded to overcome them.

I have not systematically studied the motivation of members of liberation movements. My comments on motives are, therefore, based mainly on introspection and on observation of social justice activists, including radical social workers, with whom I have been associated. Based on this, I think that searching for meaning in one's life is an important motive which enables many people to overcome their dilemmas and hesitation concerning struggles for social justice.

Once people attain critical consciousness and come to understand the sources and dynamics of injustice and oppression, and realize that, directly or indirectly, they and their families are also caught in these dynamics, which they can no longer disregard, they are likely to feel compelled to challenge them unless they are ready to live a constant lie. Their sense of having to act is spurred not only by their awareness of the unmet needs of severely oppressed people, but also by their own insecurity and by the continuous frustration of their own real human needs and interests.

Upon becoming involved in movements working for human survival by trying to reverse the vicious circle of structural violence, which leads to injustice and growing inequalities, people are likely to discover new meaning in their lives, in spite of the existential dilemmas associated with their efforts. They may also derive a sense of contentment, when realizing that they are no longer trapped in, and fooled by, the dynamics and illusions of the dominant culture. Furthermore, they may experience rewarding human relations and a sense of community with individuals with whom they work for social justice, and with whom they might create "liberated space," and alternative, cooperative institutions, prefiguring future egalitarian social relations, from within the established hierarchical social order. Commitment to activism for social justice, motivated by the search for meaning, is, however, unlikely to be free from ambivalence. Rather, doubts and dilemmas may continue along with, and in spite, of commitment.

Another motive for overcoming the existential dilemmas are an individual's belief system. People with a strong belief in a religious faith may be helped to overcome their dilemmas by accepting the ethical imperatives and values of their faith. Similarly, people who adopt a secular belief system, such as a commitment to the survival and development of all people, everywhere, are also likely to be helped to transcend their dilemmas by accepting humanist ethics and values.

It follows that people, motivated by a search for meaning and by ethical imperatives and values, have often overcome the existential dilemmas which affect the readiness to confront the root causes of injustice and oppression, and that they can, and will, do so again, now and in the future. We cannot know, however, whether people who overcome their dilemmas and join movements for social justice will mobilize sufficient energy and resources, and will develop strategies effective enough to reverse prevailing destructive trends toward the intensification of inequalities, injustice, and oppression all over the globe.

Scholarly analyses of current human realities and tendencies are not encouraging, though they reveal also the feasibility of moving toward sustainable, social and economic, global futures. Rather than becoming paralyzed by negative scenarios predicted by analysts, social justice activists, including social workers committed to their ethical mandate, need to intensify their struggles against the causes of injustice and oppression in order to increase the probability of avoiding the self-destruction of the human species, and to realize the scenarios of sustainability, also projected by analysts. Antonio Gramsci's answer to the existential dilemmas, while jailed under fascism in Italy for his commitment to social justice and human equality, seems as sound a guide for present global realities, as it was in Gramsci's difficult time:

> Pessimism of the mind;
> Optimism of the will (Hoare and Smith 1971).

APPENDIX A

An Economic Bill of Rights

Proposed by President Franklin Delano Roosevelt, State of the Union Message, January 11, 1944

This republic had its beginning, and grew to its present strength, under the protection of certain inalienable political rights—among them the right to free speech, free press, free worship, trial by jury, freedom from unreasonable searches and seizures. They were our rights to life and liberty.

As our Nation has grown in size and stature, however—as our industrial economy expanded—these political rights proved inadequate to assure us equality in the pursuit of happiness.

We have come to a clear realization of the fact that true individual freedom cannot exist without economic security and independence. "Necessitous men are not freemen." People who are hungry and out of a job are the stuff of which dictatorships are made.

In our day these economic truths have become accepted as self-evident. We have accepted, so to speak, a second Bill of Rights under which a new basis of security and prosperity can be established for all—regardless of station, race, or creed.

Among these are:

The right to a useful and remunerative job in the industries, or shops or farms or mines of the Nation;

The rights to earn enough to provide adequate food and clothing and recreation;

The right of every farmer to raise and sell his products at a return which will give him and his family a decent living;

The right of every businessman, large and small, to trade in an atmosphere of freedom from unfair competition and domination by monopolies at home and abroad;

The right of every family to a decent home;

The right to adequate medical care and the opportunity to achieve and enjoy good health;

The right to adequate protection from the economic fears of old age, sickness, accident, and unemployment;

The right to a good education;

All of these rights spell security. And after this war is won, we must be prepared to move forward, in the implementation of these rights, to new goals of human happiness and well-being.

APPENDIX B

The Universal Declaration of Human Rights

Adopted by the United Nations on December 10, 1948

Preamble

Whereas recognition of the inherent dignity and of the equal and inalienable rights of all members of the human family is the foundation of freedom, justice, and peace in the world,

Whereas disregard and contempt for human rights have resulted in barbarous acts which have outraged the conscience of mankind, and the advent of a world in which human beings shall enjoy freedom of speech and belief and freedom from fear and want has been proclaimed as the highest aspiration of the common people,

Whereas it is essential, if man is not to be compelled to have recourse, as a last resort, to rebellion against tyranny and oppression, that human rights should be protected by the rule of law,

Whereas it is essential to promote the development of friendly relations between nations,

Whereas the peoples of the United Nations have in the Charter reaffirmed their faith in fundamental human rights, in the dignity and worth of the human person and in the equal rights of men and women and have determined to promote social progress and better standards of life in larger freedom,

Whereas Member States have pledged themselves to achieve, in cooperation with the United Nations, the promotion of universal respect for the observance of human rights and fundamental freedoms,

Whereas a common understanding of these rights and freedoms is of the greatest importance for the full realization of this pledge,

Now, Therefore, The General Assembly Proclaims

This Universal Declaration of HumanRights

as a common standard of achievement of all peoples and all nations, to the end that every individual and every organ of society, keeping this Declaration constantly in mind, shall strive by teaching and education to promote respect for the rights and freedoms and by progressive measures, national and international, to secure their universal and effective recognition and observance, both among the peoples of Member States themselves and among the peoples of territories under their jurisdiction.

Article 1. All human beings are born free and equal in dignity and rights. They are endowed with reason and conscience and should act towards one another in a spirit of brotherhood.

Article 2. Everyone is entitled to all the rights and freedoms set forth in this Declaration, without distinction of any kind, such as race, colour, sex, language, religion, political or other opinion, national or social origin, property, birth, or other status.

Furthermore, no distinction shall be made on the basis of the political, jurisdictional or international status of the country or territory to which a person belongs, whether it be independent, trust, self-governing or under any other limitation of sovereignty.

Article 3. Everyone has the right to life, liberty, and security of person.

Article 4. No one shall be held in slavery or servitude; slavery and the slave trade shall be prohibited in all their forms.

Article 5. No one shall be subjected to torture or to cruel, inhuman or degrading treatment or punishment.

Article 6. Everyone has the right to recognition everywhere as a person before the law.

Article 7. All are equal before the law and are entitled without any discrimination to equal protection of the law. All are entitled to equal protection against discrimination in violation of this Declaration and against any incitement to such discrimination.

Article 8. Everyone has the right to an effective remedy by the competent national tribunals for acts violating the fundamental rights granted him by the constitution or law.

Article 9. No one shall be subjected to arbitrary arrest, detention or exile.

Article 10. Everyone is entitled in full equality to a fair and public hearing by an independent and impartial tribunal, in the determination of his rights and obligations and of any criminal charge against him.

Article 11. (1) Everyone charged with a penal offense has the right to be presumed innocent until proven guilty according to law in a public trial at which he has had all the guarantees necessary for his defense.

(2) No one shall be held guilty of any penal offense on account of any act or omission which did not constitute a penal offense, under national or international law, at the time when it was committed. Nor shall a heavier penalty be imposed than the one that was applicable at the time the penal offense was committed.

Article 12. No one shall be subjected to arbitrary interference with his privacy, family, home, or correspondence, nor to attacks upon his honor and reputation. Everyone has the right to protection of the law against such interference or attacks.

Article 13. (1) Everyone has the right to freedom of movement and residence within the borders of each State.

(2) Everyone has the right to leave any country, including his own, and to return to his country.

Article 14. (1) Everyone has the right to seek and to enjoy in other countries asylum from persecution.

(2) This right may not be invoked in the case of persecutions genuinely arising from non-political crimes or from acts contrary to the purposes and principles of the United Nations.

Article 15. (1) Everyone has the right to a nationality.

(2) no one shall be arbitrarily deprived of his nationality nor denied the right to change his nationality.

Article 16. (1) Men and women of full age, without limitation due to race, nationality or religion, have the right to marry and to found a family. They are entitled to equal rights as to marriage, during marriage and at its dissolution.

(2) Marriage shall be entered into only with the free and full consent of the intending spouses.

(3) The family is the natural and fundamental group unit of society and is entitled to protection by society and the State.

Article 17. (1) Everyone has the right to own property alone as well as in association with others.

(2) No one shall be arbitrarily deprived of his property.

Article 18. Everyone has the right to freedom of thought, conscience and religion; this right includes freedom to change his religion or belief, and freedom, either alone, or in community with others and in public or private, to manifest his religion or belief in teaching, practice, worship and observance.

Article 19. Everyone has the right to freedom of opinion and expression; this right includes freedom to hold opinions without interference and to seek, receive and impart information and ideas through any media and regardless of frontiers.

Article 20. (1) Everyone has the right to freedom of peaceful assembly and association.

(2) No one may be compelled to belong to an association.

Article 21. (1) Everyone has the right to take part in the government of his country, directly or through freely chosen representatives.

(2) Everyone has the right of equal access to public service in his country.

(3) The will of the people shall be the basis of the authority of government; this will shall be expressed in periodic and genuine elections which shall be by universal and equal suffrage and shall be held by secret vote or by equivalent free voting procedure.

Article 22. Everyone, as a member of society, has the right to social security and is entitled to realization, through national effort and international co-operation and in accordance with the organization and resources of each State, of the economic, social and cultural rights indispensable for his dignity and the free development of his personality.

Article 23. (1) Everyone has the right to work, to free choice of employment, to just and favorable conditions of work and to protection against unemployment.

(2) Everyone, without discrimination, has the right to equal pay for equal work.

(3) Everyone who works has the right to just and favorable remuneration ensuring for himself and family an existence worthy of human dignity, and supplemented, if necessary, by other means of social protection.

(4) Everyone has the right to form and to join trade unions for the protection of his interests.

Article 24. Everyone has the right to rest and leisure, including reasonable limitation of working hours and periodic holidays with pay.

Article 25. (1) Everyone has the right to a standard of living adequate for the health and well-being of himself and his family, including food, clothing, housing and medical care and necessary social services, and the right to security in the event of unemployment, sickness, disability, widowhood, old age or other lack of livelihood in circumstances beyond his control.

(2) Motherhood and childhood are entitled to special care and assistance. All children, whether born in or out of wedlock, shall enjoy the same social protection.

Article 26. (1) Everyone has the right to education. Education shall be free, at least in the elementary and fundamental stages. Elementary education shall be compulsory. Technical and professional education shall be made generally available and higher education shall be equally accessible to all on the basis of merit.

(2) Education shall be directed to the full development of the human personality and to the strengthening of respect for human rights and fundamental freedoms. It shall promote understanding, tolerance and friendship among all nations, racial or religious groups, and shall further the activities of the United Nations for the maintenance of peace.

(3) Parents have a prior right to choose the kind of education that shall be given to their children.

Article 27. (1) Everyone has the right freely to participate in the cultural life of the community, to enjoy the arts and to share in scientific advancement and its benefits.

(2) Everyone has the right to the protection of the moral and mate-

rial interests resulting from any scientific, literary or artistic production of which he is the author.

Article 28. Everyone is entitled to a social and international order in which the rights and freedoms set forth in this Declaration can be fully realized.

Article 29. (1) Everyone has duties to the community in which alone the free and full development of his personality is possible.

(2) In the exercise of his rights and freedoms, everyone shall be subject only to such limitations as are determined by law solely for the purpose of securing due recognition and respect for the rights and freedoms of others and of meeting the just requirements of morality, public order and the general welfare in a democratic society.

(3) These rights and freedoms may in no case be exercised contrary to the purposes and principles of the United Nations.

Article 30. Nothing in this Declaration may be interpreted as implying for any State, group or persons any right to engage in any activity or to perform any act aimed at the destruction of any of the rights and freedoms set forth herein.

APPENDIX C

Framework for Analysis and Development
of Social Policies

Section A: Issues dealt with by the policy

1. nature, scope, and distribution of issues
2. causal theories or hypotheses concerning the issues

Section B: Objectives, value premises, theoretical positions, target segments, and substantive effects

1. overt and covert policy objectives
2. explicit and implicit value premises and ideological orientations underlying the policy objectives
3. theories and hypotheses underlying the strategy and provisions of the policy
4. target segments of society: sizes and characteristics
5. short- and long-range effects of the policy on target and nontarget segments of society:
   a. intended effects and extent of attainment of policy objectives
   b. unintended effects
   c. overall costs and benefits

Section C: Implications of the policy for the operating and outcome variables of policy systems

1. changes in the development, management, and conservation of natural and human-created resources
2. changes in the organization of work and production
3. changes in the exchange and distribution of goods and services, and of social, civil, and political rights and responsibilities
4. changes in processes of governance and legitimation
5. changes concerning reproduction, socialization, and social control
6. consequences of changes of the operating variables for:

   a. circumstances of living of individuals, groups, and classes
   b. power of individuals, groups, and classes
   c. quality of human relations among individuals, groups, and classes
   d. overall quality of life

Section D: Interactions of the policy with forces affecting life in society

1. history of the policy's development and implementation
2. political groups promoting or resisting the policy
3. attributes of the natural environment and changes in it
4. attributes and tendencies of people
5. basic and perceived needs of people
6. demographic developments in relation to natural and human-created resources
7. economic surplus and its disposition
8. differentiations and conflicts within society

   a. social, occupational, and spatial differentiations;
   b. differentiations of rights and perceptions of interests;
   c. class structure and class consciousness;
   d. conflicts concerning resources, work, rights, and the disposition of the economic surplus;

9. development of ideas, knowledge, science, and technology
10. symbolic universe and consciousness:

   a. images of established ways of life;
   b. customs and traditions;

      c. systems of ideas, beliefs, and meanings;

      d. conventional wisdom;

      e. perceptions of needs and interests;

      f. value positions and ideology

11. critical consciousness and alternative visions

12. interactions with other societies and exposure to alternative ways of life and consciousness

13. social and foreign policies relevant to the issues addressed by the policy

Section E: Development of alternative social policies:

1. specification of alternative social policies

      a. aimed at the same policy objectives, but involving alternative measures

      b. aimed at different policy objectives concerning the same policy issues

2. comparison and evaluation: each alternative policy is to be analyzed in accordance with relevant sections of the framework and compared with the original policy and other alternative policies

Source: David G. Gil. 1992. *Unravelling Social Policy*, 5th ed. Rochester, Vt.: Schenkman Books.

BIBLIOGRAPHY

Alexander, Chauncy A. 1996. "Distinctive Dates in Social Welfare History." In Richard L. Edwards, editor-in-chief, *Encyclopedia of Social Work*, 19th ed. Washington, D.C.: NASW Press.

Andrews, Janice and Michael Reisch. 1996. "The Legacy of McCarthyism on Social Work: A Historical Analysis." Paper presented at the *Annual Program Meeting of the Council on Social Work Education*, Washington, D.C., February 1996.

Applebaum, Herbert. 1992. *The Concept of Work: Ancient, Medieval, and Modern*. Albany: State University of New York.

Axinn, June and Herman Levin. 1982. *Social Welfare: A History of the American Response to Need*. 2d ed. New York: Harper and Row.

Bailey, Roy and Mike Brake, eds. 1976. *Radical Social Work*. New York: Pantheon.

Barry, Brian. 1973. *The Liberal Theory of Justice*. London: Oxford University Press.

Bentley, George R. 1970. *A History of the Freedmen's Bureau*. New York: Octagon Books.

Berger, Peter L. and Thomas Luckman. 1966. *The Social Construction of Reality*. Garden City, N.Y.: Doubleday.

Blum, Fred H. 1968. *Work and Community*. London: Routledge & Kegan Paul.

Boff, Leonardo. 1986. *Liberation Theology*, San Francisco: Harper.

Bombyk, Marti. 1995. "Progressive Social Work." In Richard L. Edwards, editor-in-chief, *Encyclopedia of Social Work.* 19th ed. Washington, D.C.: NASW Press.

Brenner, Harvey. 1984. *Estimating the Effects of Economic Change on National Health and Wellbeing.* Washington, D.C.: U.S. Government Printing Office.

Brieland, Donald. 1995. "Social Work Practice: History and Evolution." In Richard L. Edwards, editor-in-chief. *Encyclopedia of Social Work.* 19th ed. Washington, D.C.: NASW Press.

Bruyn, Severin T. and Paula M. Rayman. 1979. *Nonviolent Action and Social Change.* New York: Irvington Publishers.

Buber, Martin. 1958. *Paths in Utopia.* Boston: Beacon Press

Burns, Eveline M. 1968. *Children's Allowances and the Economic Welfare of Children.* New York: Citizens' Committee for Children of New York.

Burstow, Bonnie. 1991. "Freirian Codification and Social Work Education." *Journal of Social Work Education* 27, no. 2.

Carson, Mina Julia. 1990. *Settlement Folk: Social Thought and the American Settlement Movement, 1885–1930.* Chicago: University of Chicago Press.

Cloward, Richard A. and Frances Fox Piven. 1992. "The Myth of Dependence." *Democratic Left* 20(4) (July/August): 5–6.

Collins, Sheila D., Helen Lachs Ginsburg, Gertrude Schaffner Goldberg, 1994. *Jobs for All: A Plan for the Vitalization of America.* New York: Apex Press.

Corrigan, Paul and Peter Leonard. 1978. *Social Work Practice Under Capitalism.* London: Macmillan.

CSWE (Council on Social Work Education). 1994. *Curriculum Policy Statement.* Washington, D.C.: CSWE.

Crunden, Robert Morse. 1982. *Ministers of Reform: The Progressive's Achievements in American Civilization, 1889–1920.* New York: Basic Books.

Davis, Allen Freeman. 1967. *Spearheads of Reform: The Social Settlements and the Progressive Movement, 1890–1914.* New York: Oxford University Press.

Dewey, John. 1935. *Liberalism and Social Action.* New York: Putnam.

Durant, Will. 1935. *The Story of Civilization.* Vol 1: *Our Oriental Heritage.* New York: Simon and Schuster.

Ehrenreich, John H. 1985. *The Altruistic Imagination: A History of Social Work and Social Policy in the United States.* Ithaca, N.Y.: Cornell University Press.

Eisler, Riane. 1987. *The Chalice and the Blade.* New York: Harper and Row.

Farb, Peter. 1968. *Man's Rise to Civilization.* New York: Avon.

Fellowship for Intentional Community and Communities Publication Cooperative. 1990. *Intentional Communities—1990/91 Directory.* Evansville, Ind.: Fellowship for Intentional Community, and Stelle, Ill.: Communities Publication Cooperative.

Fisher, Jacob. 1980. *The Response of Social Work to the Depression.* Cambridge, Mass.: Schenkman.

Frank, Andre Gunder. 1977. *World Accumulation 1492–1789.* New York: Monthly Review Press.

Freire, Paulo. 1973. *Education for Critical Consciousness,* New York: Seabury Press.

——. 1970. *Pedagogy of the Oppressed.* New York: Herder and Herder.

Freud, Sigmund. 1938. *Basic Writings,* ed. A. A. Brill. New York: Modern Library, Random House.

——. 1959. *Collected Papers.* New York: Basic Books.

Fromm, Erich. 1973. *The Anatomy of Human Destructiveness.* New York: Holt, Reinhart, and Winston.

——. 1955. *The Sane Society.* Greenwich, Conn.: Fawcett.

Galper, Jeffrey. 1980. *Social Work Practice: A Radical Perspective.* Englewood Cliffs, N.J.: Prentice-Hall.

Garraty, John A. and Peter Gay, eds. 1972. *The Columbia History of the World.* New York: Harper and Row.

Gil, David G. 1970. *Violence Against Children.* Cambridge: Harvard University Press.

——. 1974. "Practice in Human Services as a Political Act." *Journal of Clinical Child Psychology,* 3(1) (Winter–Spring): 15–20.

——. 1976. *The Challenge of Social Equality.* Cambridge, Mass.: Schenkman.

——. 1978. "Clinical Practice and Politics of Human Liberation." *Catalyst* 1, no.2.

——. 1979. *Beyond the Jungle.* Cambridge, Mass.: Schenkman; Boston: G. K. Hall.

——. 1983. "100 x 8 = 114.3 x 7 or How to Lick Unemployment." *The Humanist Sociologist* 8, no. 2 (June).

——. 1986. "Toward Constitutional Guarantees of Employment and Income," *Humanity and Society* 10, no. 2 (May).

——. 1987. "Human Services and Human Liberation: Notes on Practice and Education." *Journal of Teaching in Social Work* 1, no. 2 (Fall/Winter).

——. 1992. *Unravelling Social Policy.* 5th ed. Rochester, Vt.: Schenkman.

——. 1994. "Confronting Social Injustice and Oppression." In Frederic G. Reamer, ed., *The Foundation of Social Work Knowledge.* New York: Columbia University Press.

——. 1995. "Full Employment: The Supreme Law of the Land." *Uncommon Sense.* Part 6. New York: National Jobs for All Coalition.

——. 1996. "Preventing Violence in a Structurally Violent Society: Mission Impossible." *American Journal of Orthopsychiatry* 66(1) (January):77–84.

Gil, David G. and Eva A. Gil, eds. 1987. *The Future of Work.* Cambridge, Mass.: Schenkman.

Gorz, Andre. 1967. *Strategy for Labor.* Boston: Beacon Press.

Gutierrez, Gustavo. 1973. *A Theology of Liberation History, Politics, and Salvation*. Maryknoll, N.Y.: Orbis Books.

Harvey, Philip. 1989. *Securing the Right to Employment*. Princeton: Princeton University Press.

Hoare, Quinton and Geoffrey Nowell Smith, eds. 1971. *Selections from the Prison Notebooks of Antonio Gramsci*. New York: International Publishers.

Hofstadter, Richard. 1955. *The Age of Reform: From Bryan to F.D.R*. New York: Knopf.

Hunt, E.K. and Howard J. Sherman. 1986. *Economics*. 5th ed. New York: Harper and Row.

IFSW (International Federation of Social Workers). 1994. *International Declaration of Ethical Principles of Social Work*. Oslo, Norway: IFSW.

———.1994. *International Standards for Social Workers*. Oslo, Norway: IFSW.

John Paul II. 1982. *On Human Work—Laborem Excercens*. Boston: Daughters of St. Paul.

Kanter, Rosabeth Moss. 1972. *Commitment and Community*. Cambridge: Harvard university Press.

———. 1973. *Communes: Creating and Managing the Collective Life*. New York: Harper and Row.

Katz, Michael B. 1986. *In the Shadow of the Poor House: A Social History of Welfare in America*. New York: Basic Books.

———. 1989. *The Undeserving Poor*. New York: Pantheon Books.

King, Martin Luther, Jr. 1992. *I Have a Dream: Writings and Speeches that Changed the World*. San Francisco: Harper.

Kropotkin, Petr. 1956. *Mutual Aid*. Boston: Porter Sargent.

Lakey, George. 1987. *Powerful Peacemaking: A Strategy for a Living Revolution*. Philadelphia: New Society Publishers.

Lindenfeld, Frank and Joice Rothschild-Whitt, eds. 1982. *Workplace Democracy and Social Change*. Boston: Porter Sargent.

Lorenz, Konrad. 1966. *On Aggression*. London: Methuen.

Lowell, Josephine Shaw. 1884. *Public Relief and Private Charity*. New York: Putnam.

Lubove, Roy. 1968. *The Professional Altruist: The Emergence of Social Work as a Career 1880–1930*. Cambridge: Harvard University Press.

Lundblad, Karen Shafer. 1995. "Jane Addams and Social Reform: A Role Model for the 1990s." *Social Work* 40, no. 5 (September).

Magdoff, Harry. 1977. *Imperialism: From the Colonial Age to the Present*. New York: Monthly Review Press

Marx, Karl. 1977. *Capital*. New York: Vintage Books.

Maslow, Abraham H. 1970. *Motivation and Personality*. New York: Harper and Row.

Maslow, Abraham H. and John J. Honigman. 1970. "Synergy: Some Notes of Ruth Benedict." *American Anthropologist* 72 (April): 320–333.

McLuhan, Marshall. 1967. *The Medium Is the Message*. New York: Bantam.

Mencher, Samuel. 1967. *Poor Law to Poverty Program*. Pittsburgh: University of Pittsburgh Press.

Montague, Ashley M. F., ed. 1968. *Man and Aggression*. New York: Oxford University Press.

Morgan, Robin, ed. 1970. *Sisterhood Is Powerful: An Anthology of Writings from the Women's Liberation Movement*. New York: Vintage Books.

Morrison, Roy. 1991. *We Build the Road As We Travel: Mondragon, A Cooperative Social System*. Philadelphia: New Society Publishers.

Mullaly, Robert P. and Eric F. Keating. 1991. "Similarities, Differences, and Dialectics of Radical Social Work." *Journal of Progressive Human Services* 2, no, 2.

Murray, Charles. 1984. *Losing Ground: American Social Policy 1950– 1980*. New York: Basic Books.

NASW (National Association of Social Workers). *Code of Ethics*, 1996. Washington, D.C.: NASW.

NCCB (National Conference of Catholic Bishops). 1986. *Economic Justice for All*. Washington, D.C.: NCCB.

Piven, Frances Fox and Richard A. Cloward. 1971, 1994. *Regulating the Poor: The Functions of Public Welfare*. New York: Pantheon.

Polanyi, Karl. 1944, 1957. *The Great Transformation*. Boston: Beacon Press.

Popple, Philip R. 1995. "Social Work Profession: History." In Richard L., Edwards, editor-in-chief,. *Encyclopedia of Social Work*. 19th ed. Washington, D.C: NASW Press.

Ravo Nick. 1996. "Nation's Index of Well-Being Is at Lowest in 25 Years." *New York Times*, October 14.

Rawls, John. 1971. *A Theory of Justice*. Cambridge, Mass.: Harvard University Press.

Reid, P. Nelson. 1995. "Social Welfare History." In Richard L. Edwards, editor-in-chief, *Encyclopedia of Social Work*. 19th ed. Washington, D.C.: NASW Press.

Rein, Martin. 1970. "Social Work in Search of a Radical Profession." *Social Work* 15, no. 2.

Reynolds, Bertha C. 1964. *An Uncharted Journey*. Hebron, Conn.: Practitioners Press.

Rodgers, Daniel T. 1979. *The Work Ethic in Industrial America*. Chicago: University of Chicago Press.

Rothman, David J. 1971. *The Discovery of the Asylum: Order and Disorder in the New Republic*. Boston: Little, Brown.

Rousseau, Jean-Jacques. 1967. *The Social Contract and Discourse on the Origin of Inequality*. New York: Washington Square Press, Pocket Books.

Ryan, William. 1971. *Blaming the Victim*. New York: Pantheon.

Sharp, Gene. 1973. *The Politics of Nonviolent Action*. Boston: Porter Sargent.

———. 1979. *Gandhi As A Political Strategist*. Boston: Porter Sargent.

Schor, Juliet B. 1992. *The Overworked American; The Unexpected Decline of Leisure*. New York: Basic Books.

Simple Living Collective, American Friends Service Collective, San Francisco. 1977. *Taking Charge*. New York: Bantam Books.

Skocpol, Theda. 1992. *Protecting Soldiers and Mothers: The Political Origins of Social Policy in the United States*. Cambridge: Harvard University Press.

Smith, Adam. 1961. *The Wealth of Nations*. Indianapolis: Bobbs-Merrill.

Smith, Rolland F. 1996. "Settlements and Neighborhood Centers." In Richard L. Edwards, editor-in-chief, *Encyclopedia of Social Work*. 19th ed. Washington, D.C.: NASW Press.

Sommer Constance. 1993. "Congress Again Asked to Put Price on Cooking, Diapering." *Los Angeles Times*, March 25.

Spiro, Melford E. 1970. *Kibbutz—Venture in Utopia*. New York: Schocken Books.

Storr, Anthony. 1968. *Human Aggression*. New York: Atheneum.

Tawney, R. H. 1964 [1931]. *Equality*. London: Allen and Unwin.

Theodorson, George A. and Achilles G. Theodorson. 1969. *A Modern Dictionary of Sociology*. New York: Crowell.

Thompson, David J. 1994. "Co-operation In America." *Cooperative Housing Journal*.

Thompson, Edward Palmer. 1963. *The Making of the English Working Class*. New York: Vintage Books.

Towle, Charlotte. 1945. *Common Human Needs*. Washington, D.C.: Federal Security Agency, Social Security Board.

Trattner, Walter I. 1984. *From Poor Law to Welfare State: A History of Social Welfare in America*. 3d ed. New York: Free Press.

Tucker, Robert C., ed. 1978. *The Marx-Engels Reader*. 2d ed. New York: Norton.

United Nations Center for Human Rights. 1992. *Teaching and Learning About Human Rights: A Manual for Schools of Social Work and the Social Work Profession*. New York: United Nations.

U.S. Department of Labor. 1967. *Three Standards of Living*, (Bulletin No. 1570–5). Washington, D.C.: U.S. Government Printing Office.

van Kleeck, Mary. 1991. "Our Illusions Concerning Government." *Journal of Progressive Human Services* 2, no. 1.

Wagner, David. 1989. "Radical Movements in the Social Services: A Theoretical Framework." *Social Service Review* 63, no. 2.

Wenocur, Stanley and Michael Reisch. 1989. *From Charity to Enterprise: The Development of American Social Work in a Market Economy*. Champaign: University of Illinois Press.

Wilensky, Harold and Charles N. Lebeaux. 1958. *Industrial Society and Social Welfare*. New York: Russell Sage Foundation.

Wineman, Steven. 1984. *The Politics of Human Services: Radical Alternatives to the Welfare State*. Boston: South End Press.

Withorn, Ann. 1984. *Serving the People: Social Services and Social Change*. New York: Columbia University Press.

Wronka, Joseph. 1992. *Human Rights and Social Policy in the 21st Century*. Lanham, Md.: University Press of America.

Zinn, Howard. 1980. *A People's History of the United States*. New York: Harper and Row.

INDEX